IMAGES
of America

NEW YORK CITY
POLICE

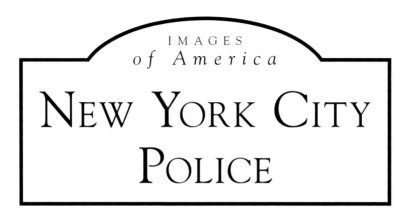

IMAGES
of America

NEW YORK CITY
POLICE

Joshua Ruff and Michael Cronin for
The New York City Police Museum
Foreword by
Police Commissioner Raymond W. Kelly

ARCADIA
PUBLISHING

Published by Arcadia Publishing
Charleston, South Carolina

Printed in the United States of America

Library of Congress Control Number: 2011925435

For all general information, please contact Arcadia Publishing:
Telephone 843-853-2070
Fax 843-853-0044
E-mail sales@arcadiapublishing.com
For customer service and orders:
Toll-Free 1-888-313-2665

Visit us on the Internet at www.arcadiapublishing.com

CONTENTS

FOREWORD

The history of the New York City Police Department reflects the history of New York City itself—dramatic, dynamic, colorful, and inspiring in countless ways. I commend The New York City Police Museum and the authors of this book for undertaking the ambitious effort to document, in words and images, the story of one of the world's greatest law enforcement traditions.

What began in 1845 with a few hundred men, predominantly Irish immigrants, has become the largest and most diverse municipal police force in the United States. Today, there are 50,000 uniformed and civilian men and women of every conceivable faith and ethnicity who keep the police department running smoothly and patrol the city's streets, subways, and housing developments. Together, they have achieved historic gains in public safety and made the NYPD a global model for policing.

The past 167 years have witnessed many challenges, from political, economic, and social upheaval to the explosion of the illegal narcotics trade and the terrorist attacks of September 11, 2001. This book chronicles those challenges and the measures the police department took to confront them. What emerges is the picture of a remarkably resilient organization that has adapted time and again to the changes in the city and world around it.

There is, of course, one other constant to which the NYPD owes its success more than anything else: the timeless courage and heroism of police officers who put themselves in harm's way to protect the public. Every day, our officers are making outstanding contributions to the city's safety and writing the next chapter of the department's history.

Sincerely,
Raymond W. Kelly
Police Commissioner

ACKNOWLEDGMENTS

There were many, many people who made this volume possible. To begin, we extend our gratitude to Police Commissioner Raymond W. Kelly for his thoughtful foreword to this book and the tremendous assistance provided by his team at the NYPD.

As authors, we benefited from a foundation of great work from a diverse body of historians and journalists. Volumes, such as *NYPD* (2000) by Thomas Reppetto and James Lardner and *The New York Police: Colonial Times to 1970* (1970) by James F. Richardson, helped guide some of the choices and work represented here.

And we were informed by much earlier efforts, such as the first detailed historical account of New York's police, *Our Police Protectors* (1885), by Augustine Costello and the books of three police officers turned writers that provided terrific firsthand accounts of early police work: George Washington Walling, John J. Hickey, and Cornelius Willemse. In recent decades, the city's policing history has been well preserved by retired detective first grade John Reilly (who sadly passed away several years ago), retired sergeant Mike Bosak, and Det. Mark Warren. Many of the images inside this book came from decades of careful, persistent accumulation by Det. Al Young.

We are grateful to the numerous staff members and colleagues at The New York City Police Museum who made our work possible and gave some help along the way. We also appreciate efforts of the founders of The New York City Police Museum, former Police Commissioner Howard Safir and his wife, Carol Safir. Without their unwavering commitment to the rich history of the NYPD, none of this would have been possible. Thank you also goes to the museum's dedicated board of trustees.

Our editor at Arcadia, Erin Vosgien, saw this enterprise through from its earliest stages and was a joy to work with.

Unless otherwise noted, the photographs and collection objects inside this book belong to the New York City Police Department. Many are housed at The New York City Police Museum, a remarkable institution in Lower Manhattan, which is devoted to bringing the NYPD's equally remarkable history to life.

Any and all photographs and images appearing in this book that are owned by the New York City Police Department (NYPD) and/or The New York City Police Museum (NYCPM) may not be reproduced, copied, or disseminated without the written consent of the NYPD and/or the NYCPM.

INTRODUCTION

"Night and day, fair weather and foul . . . a policeman must be prepared to meet all kinds of danger," wrote police historian Augustine Costello in 1885. Their work, he continues, is rarely understood by city residents. Few "know what a policeman really is, and what his duties, trials, temptations, responsibilities and virtues are."

While Costello's words still ring true nearly 120 years later, today's NYPD is an entirely different operation than the one he chronicled. "Police officer," not "policeman," is the current acceptable term, accounting for women's ever-increasing role in the department since the early 1970s. And the department has expanded in every measurable way since 1885, going from 2,800 officers protecting Manhattan to over 38,000 officers and spreading across an enormous city of five boroughs. Many special units and services exist within the department today that were not around in Costello's time: the Emergency Service Unit, the Aviation Unit, and the Community Affairs Bureau, to name just a few.

The breadth of change is best grasped by reviewing historic photographs. This book provides a pictorial history of New York City policing, from the 17th-century Dutch Colonial "rattle watch" to the seismic shifts experienced by both the city and the department in the aftermath of September 11, 2001. It proceeds chronologically, recounting milestones in the department's history, examining key figures, and considering technological developments. The first chapter explores the origins of policing New York right through the dissolution of the Metropolitan Police Squad in 1870. The second chapter examines an expanding mission and large-scale municipal corruption through 1905. The most dangerous time to be a New York City police officer, the Prohibition era, is covered in the third chapter. The fourth chapter spans the Great Depression and World War II years. Postwar modernization of the department through 1980 is the focus of the fifth chapter, and the last chapter encompasses the past three decades, including the metamorphosis of an organization solely focused on crime fighting to fighting crime and terrorism.

As authors, we were given a great opportunity and responsibility to provide a balanced historical portrait of what is—especially when considering its endless portrayals in television and film dramas—the world's most famous law enforcement organization. We had a great, unrivaled archive to select our images from at The New York City Police Museum. It is our hope that this little book brings further public awareness of the museum, just as it expands the historical record of the NYPD.

One

EARLY POLICING IN

NEW YORK CITY

1625–1870

In 1625, the colony of New Amsterdam was confined to the southern tip of Manhattan. The community's first law enforcement officer, Johan Lampo, was appointed as a *shout-fiscal*, a job that combined the roles of police officer and district attorney. Besides arresting fellow colonists, he administered punishments, usually the whipping post and the stocks. In 1658, eight men supplemented this post, plus a captain, known as the rattle watch, named for the wooden rattles they carried. This night-watch system would stay largely unchanged for almost 190 years.

As New York City began to grow, so did its law enforcement needs. New York's mid-19th-century growing pains included a large influx of immigrants and a surging demand for land. Crime and disorder were on the rise, especially in an area known as the "Five Points," highlighting the need for better law enforcement.

In May 1844, the legislature passed the New York City Municipal Police Act, which allowed the city to create a police force. The very next year, George Matsell was appointed the first chief of police. Matsell needed 800 men willing to work long hours for low pay. Luckily, he had a large manpower pool to draw from—Irish immigrants. The new department was given a uniform, but the men refused to wear it, claiming they were no one's "liveried lackeys." A compromise was struck, and the men wore regular clothes with a copper star attached. This is the probable derivation of the term "coppers," later shortened to "cops."

Policemen were appointed by their local aldermen, comparable to today's councilmen, for one-year terms, making their continued employment conditional. Since the police department also controlled the election process, whoever controlled the police had power over the ballot box. The Democrat-run city had more control over Manhattan's law enforcement than the state, and this did not sit well with the Republican state legislature. Thus the state legislature created a new police force, the Metropolitan Police, controlled by Albany. After Mayor Fernando Wood refused to comply, there were two separate (and rival) forces patrolling the streets of New York in the summer of 1857. Ultimately, the new force was upheld as the legal police department. The Metropolitan Police continued to serve the citizens of New York City until 1870, when the city regained control of its police.

STADT HUYS, ILLUSTRATION FROM OUR POLICE PROTECTORS, 1885. New Amsterdam was a diverse commercial entrepot from the very beginning. However, it was relatively small in size and population in the Dutch years, and its policing reflected that. Starting in the early 1650s, several groups of watchmen began to patrol city streets.

Stadt Huys

WOODEN RATTLES. The city's first police force, the rattle watch, was named for wooden rattles. When swung by the handle, it rotated and made a loud clicking sound, which was recognized by watchmen and citizens alike as a call for assistance. This was the early equivalent to the police radio.

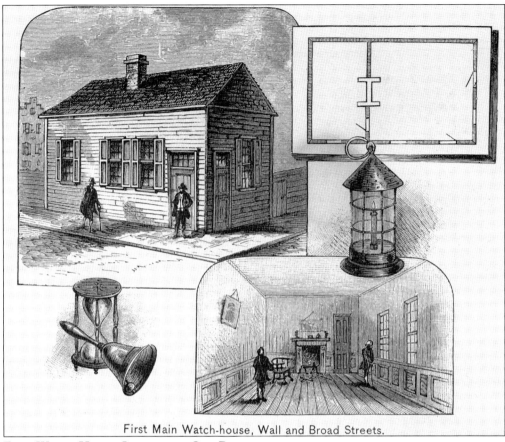

First Main Watch-house, Wall and Broad Streets.

FIRST WATCH HOUSE, IMAGE FROM *OUR POLICE PROTECTORS*. The first building constructed specifically for policing purposes in New York was a two-room, wood-frame structure, erected in 1734. The night watchmen, who patrolled from dusk to dawn, used it. Located at Broad and Wall Streets, this building also featured an outdoor cage to house prisoners as well as a whipping post and pillory for punishments. It stood until 1789.

OLD LEATHERHEAD AND SENTRY BOX, *OUR POLICE PROTECTORS*. "Leatherheads"—watchmen whose nicknames were derived from their leather helmets that protected them from the stones or bricks that often rained down from the rooftops of the city's poorer neighborhoods—got their distinctive head gear in 1827. They carried 33-inch clubs and were paid 87.5¢ per evening for their service in 1830.

Old Leatherhead and Sentry Box.

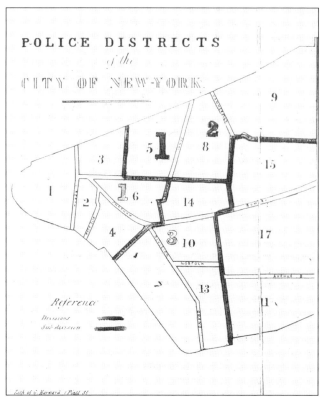

ORIGINAL POLICE DISTRICTS MAP, 1844. When the police force was formed, the plan was to divide the city into districts for supervision purposes. Mostly drawn along ward lines, the subdivisions or precincts were located within the area controlled by the alderman of that district. Not much attention was paid to what was considered the countryside at the time—the area north of Fourteenth Street.

THE OLD BREWERY, FIVE POINTS, ILLUSTRATION, C. 1850. The former brewery, forced to close once its source of water was gone, became the epicenter of the Five Points, the city's locus of vice and degradation in the 1830s and 1840s. Perhaps as many as 1,000 people at once resided in the brewery. This was the only area of the mid-19th-century city where patrolmen worked in pairs at night. Although contemporary reports of a "murder a night" here were greatly exaggerated, when the building was eventually torn down, many sets of unidentified human remains were removed.

CAPTAIN.   CAP-COVER FOR RAIN.   CHIEF.   RESERVE CORPS.   LIEUTENANT.,   PRIVATE.

NEW REGULATION UNIFORM OF THE NEW YORK POLICE.

PROPOSED UNIFORMS, 1845. When the plan for establishing a police force was developed, a uniformed force was envisioned, similar to London's "Bobbies." Unfortunately, the new policemen refused to wear them. The mostly Irish force saw uniforms as a mark of servitude. The men did agree to wear a star-shaped badge on their own street clothes. Uniforms were not introduced until 1853.

FIRST SHIELD, 1845. The New York City police's first shield was an eight-pointed star, made of stamped roofing copper. The star commemorated the first paid police force in New York, the eight rattle watchmen of 1658. The new force was initially called the "star police," after the shape of the shield, but soon picked up the nickname "coppers" from the shield's material. The term "cop" thus had its origins.

The First N.Y.P.D. Shield Design - 1845

(the shield was made of copper)

MAGEE DEL.   BRITT Sc.

JACOB HAYS, HIGH CONSTABLE OF NEW YORK

ENGRAVING OF JACOB HAYS, 1846. Considered the nation's first detective, Hays became a figure of international renown for his ability to quickly track down and apprehend criminals. He often patrolled the streets alone, armed only with a baton he used to skillful effect.

CERTIFICATE OF APPOINTMENT, 1848. Appointment to the police force was considered a step up the social ladder for many young working men, the vast majority of whom were Irish immigrants. Engraved certificates were issued to members joining the force and were often framed and proudly displayed in the officer's home. This certificate was issued to Patrolman Joseph H. Rice and signed by Mayor William Havemeyer.

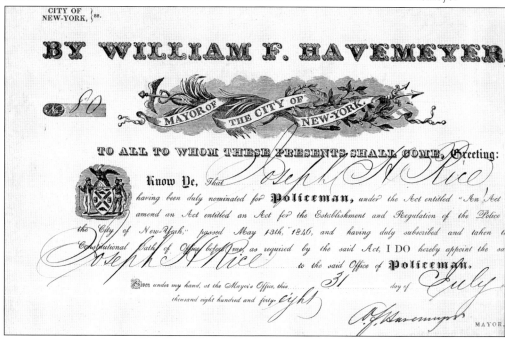

Astor Place Riot.

THE ASTOR PLACE RIOT, 1849. New York City's police squad was still in its infancy when it faced its biggest early challenge, the rioting in May 1849, outside of the Astor Place Theater. A rivalry between American actor Edward Forrest and English actor William Macready prompted a large Irish immigrant crowd of protestors demonstrating against Macready. The mob violence resulted in more than 30 deaths and 40 injuries. This incident led to the first police training in riot control and to the authorization of the first police weapon, a 22-inch-long club.

CHIEF GEORGE WASHINGTON MATSELL, 1853. George Washington Matsell was New York City's first police chief. He instituted many of the police department's early guidelines. After losing his job during the years that the Republican-controlled New York State Legislature ran the Metropolitan Police Department, Matsell briefly returned as commissioner in the 1870s.

EARLY POLICE CAPTAINS, 1856. The early years of the police department were marked by constant change as the city's new law enforcement body grew and attempted to define itself. Political orientation played a leading role in both police appointments and the department's governance. Salaries were raised annually but stayed relatively low. Captains were paid $1,000 per year by 1853.

CAPT. JOHN D. McKEE.   CAPT. MICHAEL HALFIN.   CAPT. EDWARD LETTS.
CAPT. THOMAS HANNEGAN.

FIGHT BETWEEN THE METROPOLITAN AND MUNICIPAL POLICE.

POLICE RIOT, 1857. When the state legislature passed a law seizing control of the police, the city found itself with two police forces: the Metropolitans, controlled by the state, and the Municipals, controlled by Mayor Fernando Wood. The two forces proceeded to fight one another, instead of crime. Their dispute culminated in a bloody riot on the steps of city hall. The Municipal Police Force was soon disbanded.

ILLUSTRATION OF DEAD RABBIT RIOT FROM *FRANK LESLIE'S ILLUSTRATED NEWSPAPER*, 1857. What started as a street fight between two rival gangs, the Dead Rabbits and the Bowery B'hoys, quickly changed to a citywide gang war. The police were preoccupied at the time with the conflict between the rival forces of the Municipal and Metropolitan. The militia was finally called in to restore order. (Library of Congress.)

OLD DIAL TELEGRAPH, C. 1860. Although the police department had the telegraph system very early in New York City history, its use was confined to communications between headquarters and precincts. Policemen on patrol did not have access to Morse code contact until the arrival of call boxes in the 1880s. The telegraph played a key role in deployment during the draft riots of 1863.

Escaping Rioters Surprised by the Police.

The New York City Draft Riot, 1863. Beginning on Monday, July 13, 1863, New York was overtaken by riot and mayhem due to protests of the draft to fill manpower quotas for the Union army during the Civil War. For four days, police engaged in combat with the mob using the only tool they had, their nightsticks. Among the injured was police superintendent John A. Kennedy, who was brutally beaten by a crowd. This drawing depicts the Metropolitan Police capturing escaping rioters.

Ninth Precinct.

New York July 24 1863

To the Board of Police of the Metropolitan Police District of the State of New York :

I hereby CHARGE Michael Kelly

with Improper Conduct

SPECIFICATION.

That Kelly during the week of the late Riots. commencing Monday July 13th, did not perform his duties in a Satisfactory manner, making no effort in the contests in which we were engaged, to drive back the Rioters, and was heard to remark, that his Heart was with them, (the Rioters)

Off. George Vanderbilt
" Henry I Sherman
" Henry Reynard
" Charles Simmons
" James C Chesterfield
" Alfred P Schultz
Jacob L Sebring Cap

POLICE CITATION FOR LAPSE OF DUTY DURING DRAFT RIOT, 1863. This entry documents the conflicted feelings some police officers felt about those who participated in the draft riot. It reads that the accused officer "did not perform his duties in a Satisfactory manner, making no effort in the contests in which we were engaged, to drive back the Rioters, and was heard to remark, that his Heart was with them, the Rioters."

19

METROPOLITAN POLICE HEADQUARTERS, C. 1863. When the new Metropolitan Police Force was created in 1857, they had no headquarters. The Metropolitans started construction of a building and completed their center at 300 Mulberry Street in 1863, just in time to be used as a command center for the draft riots. Theodore Roosevelt later had an office there during his stint as a police commissioner.

GROUP OF METROPOLITAN POLICE, C. 1864. This is one of the earliest uniformed group portraits taken of New York City police officers. The bottom of the picture reveals the stands their photographer used to attach to people to keep them still for the sitting.

JOHN KELLY, C. 1865. John Kelly was a leader of the department's early Harbor Unit, established in 1858. Serving aboard police boat No. 1, he was rewarded for his bravery during an oil works fire on Hunters Island. After retirement, Kelly became a riverboat captain on the Hudson River and deputy sheriff in Westchester County. (Courtesy of Bill Murray.)

TWO METROPOLITAN POLICE SQUAD OFFICERS, C. 1870. From 1857 until 1870, New York City's policing was placed in the hands of the Metropolitan Police Force, which was governed by state officials, primarily Republicans, in Albany. In 1870, police control was returned to a local board of Tammany-loyalist Democrats in New York City, after William "Boss" Tweed forced a new city charter through the state legislature.

32ND PRECINCT BUILDING, C. 1865. Located at 135th Street and Tenth Avenue, this precinct station house was on the outer edge of Manhattan's development in the 1860s, and the blotters from this precinct at this time are full of references to curtailing escaped livestock. Several horses are visible on the right side of the image; while the first mounted patrol was still a few years away, the department was using horses regularly by the 1860s to chase down criminals attempting to ride beyond city boundaries.

Two

The Challenge
of Reform
1870–1905

On April 5, 1870, the state legislature changed New York City's charter and dissolved the Metropolitan Police, thus establishing renewal of the city-controlled Municipal Police. The person most responsible for this action was Sen. William Marcy Tweed, also known as "Boss Tweed." In an ironic footnote, the same police that he reestablished arrested him three years later for corruption.

New York City after the Civil War continued to grow beyond all expectations. The city's territorial and population growth led to expanded police duties. The department became the de facto city agency, with wide-ranging responsibilities, including controlling alcohol sales, licensing steam boilers, inspecting tenement houses, street cleaning, and even housing the homeless. The department maintained homeless shelters, usually in the basements of precinct station houses.

This era of growth also became a time of widespread police corruption. Appointment to as well as promotion in the department could be bought and paid for. Payments were made to the police from gamblers, prostitution rings, and saloon keepers who wished to serve alcohol on Sundays. The outcry of some prominent citizens finally led to state senate hearings led by Clarence Lexow. The hearing's aftermath entailed the ouster of some Tammany Hall politicians and the appointment of Theodore Roosevelt.

Roosevelt was given the post of president of the Board of Police Commissioners. As president, he had no more power than any other member of the four-man board, but his sheer will and determination spearheaded a department cleanup. He personally went on midnight patrols looking for officers not on post. He pushed through reforms that laid the groundwork for the modern NYPD. New disciplinary rules, merit-based police appointments, the creation of a school for pistol practice, and the formation of a bicycle squad were just a few of the improvements made during his tenure.

The next election found Tammany back in power and Roosevelt out. Unfortunately, corruption became endemic again. The new chief of police was William S. Devery, who took grafting to new levels. While still a captain, he told his men, "If there's any grafting to be done, I'll do it. Leave it to me." Devery amassed a small fortune during his time at the top. As the 20th century opened, the new, larger city faced many battles, both from within and outside the metropolis.

OFFICERS WEARING PANAMA HATS, C. 1871. Although uniforms consisted of standard issue items, some variances were allowed. Precinct commanders at one time could determine what kind of hat was to be worn in the summer months. The commander of the 2nd Precinct in the 1870s felt that straw Panama hats would suffice.

POLICE STEAMBOAT PATROL, C. 1882. The *Patrol* was the first boat built specifically for use by the Harbor police. It had spacious accommodations and could sleep 40 officers. Harbor policemen were required to make the boat their home from Monday morning until Saturday night. The *Patrol* was also equipped with a fire pump and could be used to fight harbor fires.

DELIVERING CAPTURED ARMS AT POLICE HEAD-QUARTERS.

DELIVERING CAPTURED ARMS, ORANGE RIOT, 1871. One of the most violent insurrections in 19th-century New York City, the Orange riot, occurred during an Irish Protestant parade celebrating the Battle of the Boyne. Over 60 civilians died, and more than 100 were wounded. More than 20 policemen were hurt. Police and several state militia regiments struggled to contain the situation and faced accusations of brutality by journalists and Catholic supporters in the wake of the riot.

FLAG OF HONOR, 1872. Despite the criticism leveled at the police after the Orange riot, local civic leaders gave the department a vote of confidence by sponsoring the design of a police flag, which was to be used for annual parades and funerals of fallen officers. A chromolithograph announcing the flag was reproduced by the commission and sent to each station house across Manhattan.

25

BROADWAY SQUAD, C. 1880 AND 1859. Before the 20th century, there were few traffic regulations in New York City. People took their lives in their own hands attempting to cross one of the world's most chaotic streets while dodging horses, carts, horse-drawn wagons, and omnibuses as well as the debris these methods of transport left behind. It became the job of the Broadway Squad to help control the flow of traffic. Originally implemented along Broadway in the 1850s, the squad was later deployed at other areas of the city. The members of this elite corps were picked for their height and strength. The Broadway Squad was the forerunner of today's Traffic Control Division.

NYPD Medals. As far back as 1855, acts of bravery and heroism by police officers were recognized and rewarded with medals. There was no standard procedure for awards, and the medal process of today started around 1871. There were department "silver" and "gold" medals as well as awards sponsored by organizations and individuals. The medal at the top of the photograph is the Department Medal, or Medal of Honor, and was first issued in 1889. A new Medal of Honor (bottom of photograph) was designed by Tiffany & Co. and first issued in 1912.

© 1973 Alfred J. Young Collection, N.Y.C.

Medal for Valor, 1877. This early medal was designed by Tiffany & Co. for the Board of Police Commissioners. This shield-shaped silver medal featured a woman placing a laurel wreath on a policeman's head and was connected to a bar inscribed with the word "Valor" by an interlocking "NY." It was this "NY" symbol that former police chief William Devery borrowed when he needed a logo for his baseball team, later the New York Yankees.

Thirty-fourth Precinct Police Station, Tremont.

1925 Bathgate Ave

34TH PRECINCT POLICE STATION, 1885. This woodcut image is taken from Augustine Costello's *Our Police Protectors*. This precinct was first used by the Metropolitan Police and was constructed as the Tremont Town Hall. Costello described it as "among the most curious Police buildings in the country. It has one story and an attic, and is perched upon rocks which are covered with turf so that it has the appearance of a fortification."

GEORGE WASHINGTON WALLING, 1885. George Washington Walling's memoir, *Recollections of a New York Chief of Police* (1887), was a remarkable insider's view of the department's early years. In it, he shared vivid memories of the city's worst uprisings, including the Astor Place and draft riots. Forced into retirement during a political shake-up in the 1880s, he criticized Inspector Thomas Byrnes's methods, which he found impetuous and self-promotional.

THOMAS BYRNES, C. 1885. Often called the father of modern detective work, Byrnes was an Irish immigrant and a Civil War veteran. He rose from patrolman to sergeant, captain, inspector, and finally superintendent. He shook up the Detective Bureau upon taking charge and theatrically declared a "dead line" at Fulton Street—any crook to venture south of there would be arrested. Critics condemned his rough interrogations, known as the "third-degree." And his constant publicity mill irritated some. He was eventually forced to retire in 1895.

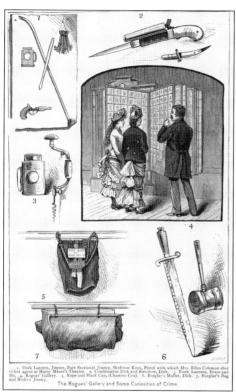

1. Dark Lantern, Jimmy, Part Sectional Jimmy, Skeleton Keys, Pistol with which Mrs. Eliza Coleman shot ticket agent at Harry Miner's Theatre. 2. Combination Dirk and Revolver, Dirk. 3. Dark Lantern, Brace and Bit. 4. Rogues' Gallery. 5. Rope and Black Cap, (Chastine Cox). 6. Burglar's Mallet, Dirk. 7. Burglar's Bag and Broken Jimmy.

The Rogues' Gallery and Some Curiosities of Crime.

ROGUES GALLERY AND WEAPONS DISPLAY, C. 1880. Using new photographic technology, Inspector Thomas Byrnes, head of the Detective Bureau, set up a display of mug shots, or photographs of criminals, in Police Headquarters to aid witnesses and victims in identifying perpetrators of crimes. The rogues gallery soon also became a popular city attraction.

POLICE TELEGRAPH OFFICE, C. 1880. The implementation of the telegraph meant far faster communications for the police. By 1854, all precinct station houses were connected to headquarters, which could be immediately notified about an emergency and could dispatch assistance quickly. The telegraph proved its worth during the draft riots as monitoring and resources were quickly deployed. This image depicts the telegraph room in the basement of the Mulberry Street headquarters.

Police Telegraph Office.

ALEXANDER WILLIAMS, C. 1885. Alexander "Clubber" Williams was a man apparently skillful both with his rhetoric and his nightstick. Originally from Nova Scotia, he rose to command the 29th Precinct and purportedly mentioned to a reporter that he was tired of "living on chuck steak in the other precincts. I will have some tenderloin now"—thus coining the neighborhood's "Tenderloin" nickname. Under extensive accusations of corruption, he was forced to retire in 1895.

Captain A. S. WILLIAMS.

Falk

949 BROADWAY, N. Y.

POLICE MATRON, 1911. Women were largely shut out of police work until the appointment of police matrons in 1891. Advocates argued that women were needed to assist the increasing number of female prisoners. The department began with four matrons and increased the number to 30 by 1896, two for each precinct. A few matrons eventually cracked into the one other area open to women at this time, the Detective Squad.

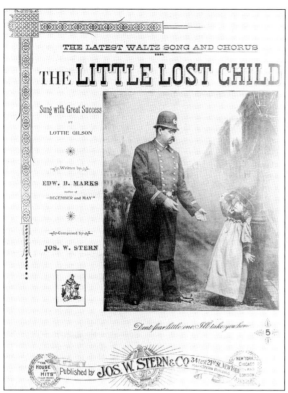

THE *LITTLE LOST CHILD*, SHEET MUSIC, JOSEPH W. STERN & COMPANY, 1899. One of the most enduring images of New York's policemen in the late 19th century was the kindly officer assisting a lost child. Although sentimentalized, the image sprang from a real social concern: the plight of orphans and abandoned children. One minister estimated Manhattan had some 10,000 children living on the streets by the 1880s, and police officers were often critical to their survival.

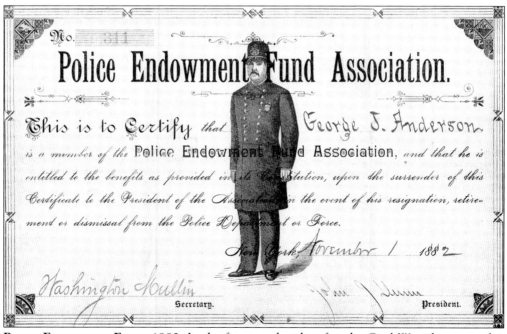

POLICE ENDOWMENT FUND, 1882. In the first two decades after the Civil War, there were few avenues of additional assistance for both retired and on-the-job police officers in New York City. Pensions became a growing concern. The Police Endowment Fund charged members a graduated amount depending on their number of years retired from the force.

UNIDENTIFIED BROOKLYN OFFICER AND FAMILY, C. 1895. The Brooklyn Police Department (prior to the 1898 consolidation) had its own pension fund, paid for by excise taxes, police penalties, and reward collections. In Manhattan, the endowment fund helped, but police families did not have much protection until 1893, when the city began collecting two percent of annual salaries to cover the costs. In 1898, the Patrolmen's Benevolent Association was founded for additional assistance.

THEODORE ROOSEVELT AT HIS DESK AT HEADQUARTERS, C. 1895. The future president of the United States was first president of the Board of Police Commissioners in New York. While he had no more legal authority than any other commissioner on this board, he acted on the strength of his character. Roosevelt would often go out on patrol at night, not looking for criminals, but looking to see if his patrolmen were doing their job.

POLICE BOARD 1896

L.S.POSNER   THEO.ROOSEVELT

ANDREW D.PARKER   COL.KIP   COL.F.D.GRANT   COL.AVERY D.ANDRE
CHIEF CLERK

POLICE BOARD, 1896. The Lexow Commission was headed by state senator Clarence Lexow of Rockland County. It was formed after allegations of widespread police department violations, including the collection of kickbacks from brothel and tavern owners. As a result of the commission's findings, a brief period of reform was initiated largely by the board seen here, which was led by Roosevelt (partially visible directly under the bookshelves, in the center).

BROOKLYN POLICE DEPARTMENT PARADE, 10TH PRECINCT, 1891. Brooklyn's Police Parade was held annually at the beginning of June. Policemen marched with their precincts with absolute precision. In 1858, a reporter described the well-choreographed scene as follows: "Blue-uniformed, white-gloved men, with brightly burnished shields on their breasts and sheathed locusts [wooden nightsticks] by their sides." The parade started at Bedford Avenue and Clymer Street and was highlighted by a stop in front of the mayor's viewing stand.

ANNUAL POLICE PARADE IN MANHATTAN, 1891. Many thousands of spectators lined the streets to show their appreciation. A reporter covering the festivities, seen in this photograph, on June 1, 1891, wrote, "If all the lawbreakers . . . could have seen the annual parade of the police force, they might have been so impressed with the physical power of this . . . agency of law and order as to have been deterred from further wrongdoing."

43RD PRECINCT GROUP PHOTOGRAPH, C. 1898. Highlighted by the presence of the station house's perky dog and a police matron, this picture was taken shortly after the city's consolidation in 1898, which was when many precinct boundaries and numbers were redrawn. This station house was at the southwest corner of Forty-third Street and Fourth Avenue. The three-story brick edifice was initially built for the 18th Precinct in 1890.

76TH PRECINCT, NORTH PRINCE STREET STATION, FLUSHING, 1904. Some of the station houses in outer-lying boroughs, in the years just after the 1898 consolidation of New York City, had a more residential feel.

CHIEF WILLIAM S. DEVERY, 1898. William "Big Bill" Devery was the last to hold the "chief of police" title. He was immortalized in the following description by journalist Lincoln Steffens: "As a Chief of Police, he is a disgrace, but as a character, he is a work of art." Under well-documented suspicion for corruption, Devery beat all charges and stayed on the job—and amassed a personal fortune. Upon retirement, he and a partner purchased a baseball club, the forerunner of the New York Yankees.

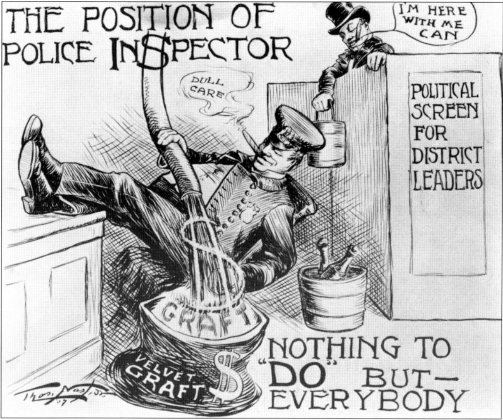

THOMAS NAST JR. CARTOON ABOUT GRAFT, 1903. Despite the reforms of the mid-1890s, Tammany Hall remained thoroughly in control of police appointments. Cops often kicked back money to their political sponsors. At the same time, a large number of policemen also extorted bribes from saloon keepers, gamblers, and prostitutes in the city's seediest areas, including the Tenderloin and the Bowery. (Courtesy of the Museum of the City of New York.)

SALOON SCENE, BROOKLYN, 1904. It was possibly a risk to the patrolman seen here when he stood for this photograph in a gas-lit Brooklyn bar. While the beat cop was responsible for everything on his post from robberies to unlocked doors at night, one place where he was not supposed to be was the neighborhood saloon. Police often entered these establishments to break up a fight or, as it was sometimes said, to arrest the winner and send the loser to the hospital.

POLICEMAN ESCORTING A MAN ON THE LOWER EAST SIDE, C. 1905. Explosive population growth and mobility provided innumerable new challenges to the police department in the early 20th century. If a person is arrested in New York today, the term the police use to describe this misfortune is "collar." This is an old term; in the days before practicable portable handcuffs, this was a common method of bringing a prisoner into the station house.

PADDY WAGON, 16TH PRECINCT, GREENPOINT AVENUE, BROOKLYN, 1901. "Paddy," or patrol, wagons may have received their moniker from the ethnic slur "paddy," referring to the Irish policemen that were operating them; it is also possible that "paddy" was indicative of the vehicle's padded interior walls. The department purchased its first of these wagons in 1886 for $500. These types of vehicles were different from the "Black Maria," which was already in use strictly to transport prisoners. Patrol wagons allowed for the rapid movement of police personnel to scenes of disorder or disaster.

MAX F. SCHMITTBERGER, C. 1905. Appointed to the department in 1874, Schmittberger rose through the ranks to eventually become chief inspector. His career was quite a bumpy ride. Once a "bag man" who made cash pick-ups for Capt. Alexander "Clubber" Williams, Schmittberger testified before the Lexow Commission and became a reformer. He was promoted to the rank of chief inspector in 1909.

Three

BATTLE FOR JUSTICE
1905–1930

After New York City's consolidation, the police department became responsible for protecting over 300 square miles of diverse boroughs, with Manhattan containing the city's financial and main business districts as well as the densely populated Lower East Side. Parts of the Bronx, Queens, and Staten Island were still sparsely populated farmlands. The department's new zone of coverage included the state's previously second largest city, Brooklyn.

There were many challenges ahead for the new police department. Traffic, in Manhattan especially, became an enormous headache. While it was always difficult to cross some streets, the addition of automobiles to the already packed avenues made the situation untenable. Since traffic signals were not fully deployed until the 1930s, sorting out the chaos became the responsibility of the NYPD's Traffic Squad.

As the city continued to grow and become more ethnically diverse, so did the NYPD. While remaining predominately Irish and German, the department began to open itself up to other ethnic groups. New Yorkers admired the great work of Lt. Joseph Petrosino and the Italian Squad in controlling the Black Hand, an aggressively dangerous new crime organization. In 1911, the NYPD hired its first African American patrolman, Samuel Battle (the old Brooklyn Police Department was the first to hire an African American officer, Wiley G. Overton, in 1891). Women also made small but significant inroads in the NYPD during this period. The first six policewomen were appointed in 1918.

In addition to a diversifying roster, the department's equipment changed. In 1905, the department deployed it first motorcycles, and by 1918, the first patrol cars were on the city streets. By 1920, the department made its entry into the radio age. The first RMPs (Radio Motor Patrol cars) were equipped with receivers only, meaning officers still had to go to call boxes to acknowledge the transmissions.

The department needed all these resources and more when the Volstead Act (better known as Prohibition) was passed in 1919. Prohibition turned out to be a boon for organized crime. Even minor criminals became kings of the illegal alcohol trade, manufacturing and distributing booze. Armored motorcycles and the Riot Squad, or Machine-gun Squad, were deployed to check increasing violence on the streets. This illegal activity led to a marked increasing risk to police officers. During the years of Prohibition, 168 members of the department lost their lives in the line of duty.

Lt. Giuseppe Petrosino, c. 1905. The department's first Italian American detective, Petrosino founded the Italian Squad and the Bomb Squad in 1903. He remains the only NYPD officer in history killed in the line of duty outside the United States. He was murdered in Palermo, Italy, in 1909, where he was gathering intelligence about the notorious Black Hand. More than 200,000 people attended Petrosino's funeral.

A ROUNDSMAN, HIS WIFE, AND TWO PATROLMAN AT BROOKLYN POLICE BOOTH, TWELFTH AVENUE AND EIGHTY-SIXTH STREET, 1908. The Bicycle Squad began at the height of interest in these vehicles nationwide in 1895. Across the city, booths were manned usually by two bicycle men connected by phone to the precinct. A police officer assigned to a booth in a rural area had many duties, including responding to calls for help from the area, monitoring speeders, and calling ahead to the next booth to apprehend motorists.

BICYCLE POLICE STOPPING CAR, C. 1909. The speed limit was eight miles per hour when these bicycle officers stopped an automobile for speeding near Grant's Tomb. The department had over 100 bicycle officers patrolling for speeders. The fine for exceeding the speed limit was $10. By 1912, the speed limit was increased to 15 miles per hour. Also increased was the officer's equipment, and the department started deploying motorcycles to combat speeders.

43

DEMONSTRATION OF NEW POLICE MOTORCYCLE LOOKING UPTOWN TOWARD FLATIRON BUILDING, c. 1905. While the Bicycle Squad was active until 1935, the department experimented and implemented its first motorcycles in 1905. The NYPD bought its first Indian motorcycles, which were then produced in Springfield, Massachusetts, in 1907. In 1920, the Motorcycle Squad was divided into three separate units: Squad No. 1 to oversee Manhattan, the Bronx, and Staten Island; Squad No. 2 was responsible for Brooklyn; and Squad No. 3 covered Queens.

ELECTRIC PATROL WAGON, c. 1910. Early motorized patrol wagons came in two varieties: gas and electric. The department determined that a gasoline wagon could cover 1,284 miles in a month, while its electric counterpart could only cover 953. This electric-powered, chain-driven wagon was one of the first non-horse-drawn vehicles in the fleet. Although electric driven, this vehicle still used kerosene lamps for illumination.

POLICE ACADEMY INSTRUCTOR REVIEWING AUTOMOBILE WITH RECRUITS, C. 1920. In the days when car ownership was the exception, rather than the rule, part of the Police Academy curriculum was the nomenclature and identification of the automobile. This photograph, taken outside Police Headquarters at 240 Centre Street, the home of the training school, shows an instructor pointing out certain aspects of the vehicle.

SAMUEL J. BATTLE, 1911. A towering presence both physically and in his strong personal character, Samuel Battle was the first African American–appointed police officer in New York City, in 1911 (Brooklyn had hired several officers prior to his appointment, but they came on before the city's consolidation). Battle bravely faced down initial discrimination from fellow police officers and civilians, earning respect and advancement through the ranks, eventually to lieutenant and parole commissioner. Battle's name is officially remembered today at the intersection of West 135th Street and Lenox Avenue in Harlem.

POLICE DEPARTMENT HEADQUARTERS, 240 CENTRE STREET, 1911. This Beaux-Arts building replaced the old Police Headquarters, which had been located at 300 Mulberry Street. Designed by Hoppin & Keon, it was a commanding and beautifully built five-story structure, made of granite and trimmed with marble and ornamental ironwork and topped by a copper dome. Stone lions flanked the front entrance. Although the structure was modern for its time, it gradually became obsolete, and in 1968, ground was broken for a new $30-million headquarters building at Park Row. After the police left the building in 1973, it remained an intact fixture in the heart of Little Italy, eventually becoming home to luxury co-op apartments.

INTERIOR VIEWS OF 240 CENTRE STREET, 1911. Principal architect Francis Hoppin claimed that he wanted "to impress both the officer and prisoner . . . with the majesty of the law." The building contained 149,530 square feet, and visitors stepped through enormous Corinthian columns at the main entrance topped with a limestone figure that represented Manhattan. Proceeding through the grand entrance hall, the headquarters featured state-of-the-art facilities, including the police surgeon's examining room, a pressroom, a pistol range, and an oval running track.

EXTERIOR OF 1ST PRECINCT BUILDING, 100 OLD SLIP, 1911. Completed in 1911 by the firm Hunt & Hunt, this structure headquartered the New York Police Department's 1st Precinct. The precinct was the launching pad for many raids on rum-running vessels along the East River waterfront during Prohibition and also protected nearby Wall Street. It later became home to the NYPD's Narcotics Squad. Since 2002, it has been home to The New York City Police Museum.

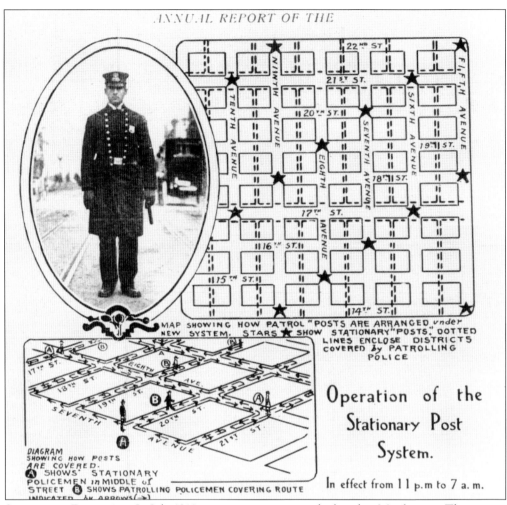

MAP SHOWING HOW PATROL "POSTS ARE ARRANGED under NEW SYSTEM. STARS ★ SHOW STATIONARY "POSTS." DOTTED LINES ENCLOSE DISTRICTS COVERED by PATROLLING POLICE

Operation of the Stationary Post System.

DIAGRAM SHOWING HOW POSTS ARE COVERED. Ⓐ SHOWS' STATIONARY POLICEMEN in MIDDLE of STREET Ⓑ SHOWS PATROLLING POLICEMEN COVERING ROUTE INDICATED by ARROWS (→)

In effect from 11 p.m to 7 a. m.

STATIONARY POST, 1911. In July 1911, stationary posts were deployed in Manhattan. These posts consisted of one set of patrolmen circulating, while another set of cops stood in the middle of the intersections, where they could be easily seen. The men in the intersections could not leave their post for any reason. The teams switched assignments every four hours. This system was discontinued when it was determined that it immobilized half the force.

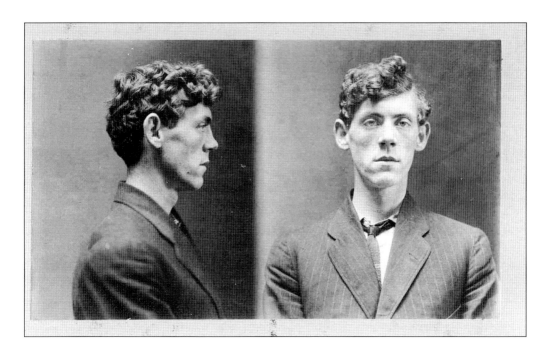

BERTILLON CARDS OF ARRESTED SUSPECTS, 1909–1912. Before the arrival of modern mug shots, the NYPD utilized a criminal identification system known as Bertillon cards, named for their creator, French police officer Alphonse Bertillon. Before the widespread use of fingerprinting, Bertillon cards used physical measurements as a key to criminal identification. The New York City Police Museum has a large collection of these cards, including the two seen here for Albert Scheu, accused of burglary in 1912, and Anna Hill, arrested for impersonating an officer in 1909.

JOHN HICKEY, C. 1910. Appointed in 1893, Patrolman John Hickey was a man of many accomplishments. He was a champion long distance runner for the department and president of the Police Athletic Association. He mentored the rookie that would become police commissioner, Richard Enright. He is best remembered for his work as an author, compiling a firsthand account of early police life in his book *Our Police Guardians.*

ELLEN O'GRADY, C. 1918. Ellen O'Grady was the first woman to serve as a deputy police commissioner for the NYPD. She was one of a small but strong cadre of women to advance in rank and impact city policing in the first decades of the 20th century. Other names to be remembered from this group include Isabelle Goodwin, the first woman to hold the title of first grade detective, and Mary Hamilton, the first director of the newly formed Policewomen's Bureau.

SHEET MUSIC, "THE FINEST," 1925.
This sheet music was for a march written
for and dedicated to the New York City
Police Band by composer Victor Herbert.
The department picked up the moniker
"The Finest" during the administration
of Mayor William Havemeyer in 1870.
The phrase caught on fast and was known
to all. This sheet music was published
by the New York City Police Band and
no doubt performed by them as well.

THE POLICE BAND, 1925. The New York City Police Band was organized in 1903 and was in great demand throughout the city, playing for most official city functions. In 1925, the band went on a nationwide tour, playing to capacity crowds. Although the band's popularity never waned, it was discontinued in February 1954 due to manpower shortages. The band was reestablished in 1991 at the urging of future Police Commissioner Raymond Kelly.

CHARLES BECKER, C. 1910, AND PAMPHLET PURPORTING BECKER'S INNOCENCE, C. 1930. Lt. Charles Becker already had a shaky past before being accused of the murder of gambler Herman Rosenthal in 1912. In 1896, he was acquitted of falsifying testimony. Later, he and a partner tried to cover up a shooting. When Rosenthal was killed, a politically ambitious district attorney, Charles Whitman, got Becker convicted of the murder and then later refused to grant him clemency as governor. Becker's widow had a silver plate attached to his coffin that read, "Charles Becker. Murdered July 30, 1915 by Governor Whitman." For years afterwards, there were questions and doubts about the extent of his role in the murder.

10 CENTS

POLICE LIEUTENANT

CHARLES BECKER

FRAMED

FOR THE

MURDER

OF

Herman Rosenthal

Here Is The Proof

JUNIOR OFFICERS, 1915. In the days before organized recreation for children, many youngsters had too much unstructured time on their hands. This sometimes led to juvenile delinquency. Capt. John S. Sweeny of the 15th Precinct organized the Junior Police to fight youth crime and give boys a purpose. The corps had boys in all ranks from patrolman to chief inspector, and all pledged to avoid bad behavior like smoking, swearing, and building bonfires.

CAMPFIRE AT SHEEPSHEAD BAY, 1918. Commissioner Richard Enright organized a nine-day encampment for 1,000 police officers at Sheepshead Bay in September 1918. The motivation for the event was to see how well the department could mobilize in a crisis situation during wartime, such as an air raid.

KUVS Radio Station, 1929. KUVS was the first police radio station to receive an operating license on June 11, 1920. The department had made earlier efforts to transmit but found that the public could hear their transmissions when using commercial frequencies.

Capt. Cornelius Willemse, 1923. This photograph from Willemse's 1931 book *Behind the Green Lights* was taken moments after a gunman had assassinated gangster Nathan "Kid Dropper" Kaplan. One of the bullets ripped through Willemse's hat. In his career, from 1899 to 1925, Willemse gained the nickname "gangbuster" and eventually became the captain of detectives. In retirement, Willemse became an important author and public lecturer on law enforcement.

PROPERTY CLERK'S OFFICE AND VAULTS BELOW POLICE HEADQUARTERS, 1928. From lost umbrellas to crime-collected and seized items, such as the gambling paraphernalia and guns visible in this picture, thousands of stories are contained in the walls of this well-known police institution. In the 1920s, all lost and seized property was held for at least six months; if unclaimed, it was generally sold with the proceeds going toward the Police Pension Fund.

OUTSIDE THE CANINE PATROL BUILDING, c. 1925. Taking a cue from similar service dogs used in Germany and Belgium, Deputy Commissioner Arthur Woods began the NYPD's canine program in 1908. Early breeds used included bloodhounds, German shepherds, and Belgian sheepdogs. Originally deployed at night, the dog would be taken to the post and let loose to patrol alleyways, behind houses, and other hiding places. Gradually, the department added more breeds and gave the dogs a wide array of responsibilities.

"Barrel Murder" Crime Scene, 1918.
In the years leading up to Prohibition, organized crime was growing increasingly violent and widespread, a problem that required enormous police resources. One of the worst mafia crimes were the so-called "barrel murders," in which the victims were brutalized and left in a barrel. In his book *Evidence* (2006), writer Luc Sante identified this crime as probably being the murder of Gaspare Candella in Brooklyn.

Ludwig Lee Escorted Out of Kings County Courthouse Building, 1927.
Ludwig Halvorsen Lee, a Norwegian immigrant, was accused of killing two women and dismembering their bodies with an axe. One of the women, Sarah Lee Brownell, was his landlady, whom he apparently murdered in a dispute over money; the other was Selma Bennett who, it was believed, was murdered to keep the crime covered up. Lee was executed in 1928.

DETECTIVE DIVISION CIRCULAR No. 9 SEPTEMBER 8, 1930	POLICE DEPARTMENT CITY OF NEW YORK	BE SURE TO FILE THIS CIRCULAR FOR REFERENCE

Police Authorities are Requested to Post this Circular for the Information of Police Officers and File a Copy of it for Future Reference.

MISSING SINCE AUGUST 6, 1930

HONORABLE JOSEPH FORCE CRATER,
JUSTICE OF THE SUPREME COURT, STATE OF NEW YORK

DESCRIPTION—Born in the United States—Age, 41 years; height, 6 feet; weight, 185 pounds; mixed grey hair, originally dark brown, thin at top, parted in middle "slicked" down; complexion, medium dark, considerably tanned; brown eyes; false teeth, upper and lower jaw, good physical and mental condition at time of disappearance. Tip of right index finger somewhat mutilated, due to having been recently crushed.

Wore brown sack coat and trousers, narrow green stripe, no vest; either a Panama or soft brown hat worn at rakish angle, size 6⅝, unusual size for his height and weight. Clothes made by Vroom. Affected colored shirts, size 14 collar, probably bow tie. Wore tortoise-shell glasses for reading. Yellow gold Masonic ring, somewhat worn; may be wearing a yellow gold, square-shaped wrist watch with leather strap.

COMMUNICATE with CHIEF INSPECTOR, POLICE DEPARTMENT, 18th Division, (Missing Persons Bureau), New York City. Telephone Spring 3100.

CIRCULAR ANNOUNCING MISSING NEW YORK STATE SUPREME COURT JUSTICE JOSEPH FORCE CRATER, 1930. On August 6, 1930, according to one version of events, 41-year-old state supreme court justice Joseph Force Crater bid his dinner companions a good evening, walked out of a West Side restaurant, climbed into a cab, and was never seen again. Police followed up on more than 3,000 leads, with claimed sightings from Cuba to Maine. Crater was declared dead in 1939, and the police department's missing person's case was closed in 1979. Recently, in 2005, papers were unearthed that suggested the judge had been the victim of a mafia hit. The case went to the Cold Case Squad but has not yet revealed any reliable conclusions.

FRANKIE YALE, C. 1925, AND THE CRIME SCENE OF YALE'S ASSASSINATION, 1928. Born Francesco Ioele in 1893, "Frankie Yale" was a member of the notorious Five Points Gang and later became Brooklyn's crime boss and mentored Al Capone. Yale was in a Brooklyn speakeasy on the morning of July 1, 1928, when he received a call that his wife was sick. The call was a ruse, and Yale's bullet-ridden Lincoln with his body inside was found on the steps of a Brooklyn home. Capone was questioned by the NYPD but was not charged.

OUTING FOR THE POLICE DEPARTMENT'S BOOKKEEPERS AND QUARTERMASTERS, 1921. Formal and informal athletic associations within the department flourished after World War I. A group of police department clerical staffers, seen here, takes a break from a friendly game of baseball under the shade of trees at the old Duers Pavilion, Whitestone Landing.

POLICE DEPARTMENT BASEBALL TEAM, C. 1930. Started at the turn of the century, the police department's baseball team played against its sports rival, the fire department. By the 1930s, many city agencies fielded teams, including the sanitation and water departments. The police held their own against most teams, until police department team members acted as ringers for the mayor's office when they played city hall reporters. Reporters trounced the mayor's team, 36-9.

POLICE DEPARTMENT
CITY OF NEW YORK

FIELD DAYS
POLICE RELIEF FUND

GRAVESEND RACE TRACK
BROOKLYN, N. Y.

GOVERNOR'S DAY—Saturday, September 10, 1921
MAYOR'S DAY—Saturday, September 17, 1921

Price 10 cents—pay no more

POLICE FIELD DAYS PROGRAM, 1921. A precursor to the Police Olympics, Field Days featured police officers participating in events such as the 1,000-yard run, 150-yard dash, and tug-of-war. Officers with 25 years or more on the job could participate but did not have to compete with the younger men. Since the proceeds supported the widows and orphans fund, organizers were pleased when Babe Ruth donated an autographed bat and glove to the person that purchased the most tickets.

MARTIN SHERIDAN, 1906. Already an Olympic gold medal winner for the discus throw, newly appointed patrolman, and recently arrived Irish immigrant, Martin Sheridan traveled to Athens for the 1906 Olympics, where he won two gold medals. He also participated in the 1908 games where he took home two more gold medals. In all, he would go on to win 51 trophies, 16 world records, and 5 gold medals. He was to get one more gold—this time a shield. Sheridan would eventually become a first grade detective. (Courtesy Winged Fist Organization.)

MATTHEW McGRATH, 1908 OLYMPICS AND NEAR HIS 1934 RETIREMENT. McGrath had participated in dozens of competitions, including four Olympiads. His event was the 16-pound hammer throw. During the parade at the 1908 Olympics in London, each team was required to lower their country's flag to salute the king. McGrath told the flag bearer, "Dip that flag and you'll be in the hospital tonight." No doubt this tenacity as well as his physical abilities helped him accumulate a collection of awards, including Olympic gold and silver medals, and to serve in the NYPD for 39 years. (Both, courtesy Winged Fist Organization.)

MOUNTED OFFICER PATROLS A SNOWY POST, C. 1930. The Mounted Police Unit was formed initially to respond to runaway saddle and carriage horses. Their effectiveness at Central Park and elsewhere led to the unit's expansion in the late 19th century. The Mounted Police Unit's crowd control abilities—they have the best vantage points and are easily spotted by the public—has given them a continued importance. Duty demands a rugged indifference to inclement weather, as this picture indicates.

POLICE ACADEMY BUILDING AT 400 BROOME STREET, C. 1930. The academy had a dizzying array of locations, with recruit classes having been held at Cooper Union in 1907. The next year, recruits began their training at Police Headquarters at 300 Mulberry Street and then, in 1911, at 240 Centre Street. After several more stops, in 1928, the academy opened its doors at this building—but this spot, too, proved to be short lived.

ARMORED MOTORCYCLES WITH SIDE CARS, 1929. The Prohibition era was a dangerous time to be a cop. Weekly newspaper reports told of bullets flying on streets, while rival gang members "shot it out." Rapid response to these shootings led to the deployment of armored motorcycles. Equipped with a sidecar and bulletproof windshield, the shotgun-armed officers had at least some protection against armed opponents.

POLICE CAR, RIFLES DRAWN AT WASHINGTON SQUARE, 1930. A large part of the department's fleet in 1930 was made up of Ford Model A's.

STINSON SR-9-A AMPHIBIAN POLICE PLANE LANDING IN WATER, 1930. The Aviation Unit took to the skies on October 24, 1929. In one prominent kidnapping case in 1931, the officers followed a homing pigeon carrying a ransom note through the air and right to the kidnapper! The relatively small air corps was gradually expanded in the 1930s and early 1940s under Mayor Fiorello LaGuardia, himself a former pilot.

Four

POLICING DURING DEPRESSION AND WARTIME
1930–1945

On December 5, 1933, Prohibition ended, and the New York City Police Department considered the results of an era of tremendous gangland violence. Despite continued danger in the early days of the Great Depression, the department benefited from an influx of highly qualified hires, talented individuals who were hard pressed to find other work. By 1941, more than half of the members of the Police Academy class were college graduates, and their starting salaries were a competitive $1,500 per year.

Mayor Fiorello LaGuardia and his trusted Police Commissioner Lewis Valentine oversaw the department during this challenging time. The duo shared longevity of office, an intolerance for corruption, and an intense antipathy toward organized crime. On his inauguration day, LaGuardia declared that Byrnes's famous "dead line" for criminals should now be extended to city limits. Valentine publicly told his detectives that they should not be afraid to "muss 'em up" and to be tougher interrogators of mafia killers. But his legacy as the NYPD's longest-serving commissioner to that point in time (1934–1945) was far more lasting than that single statement implied. Despite reduced manpower, especially during the war, under Valentine's tenure enormous amounts of weapons and gambling equipment were seized, traffic deaths declined, and the entire department's efficiency was improved.

With the start of World War II, the NYPD did its part for the nation's mobilization. The department coordinated the city's civil defense and participated in the overseas military actions. Many members of the department served in the armed forces, and those remaining in active duty in New York participated in large-scale drills, like the recreation of the Battle of Britain in Madison Square Garden. The department was also heavily involved in the Air Raid Protection Service, the City Patrol Corps, and other efforts to secure the city, with much of the supervision and coordination handled at the old Police Headquarters at 300 Mulberry Street.

On one tragic day, the NYPD saw the war come to home soil. On July 4, 1940, a bomb was found at the British Pavilion at the New York World's Fair grounds in Queens and was removed to an area where it was detonated, instantly killing two Bomb Squad detectives, Joseph Lynch and Ferdinand Socha. This terrible incident led to important new changes in the Bomb Squad, including the introduction of a steel-wire containment truck for the safer disposal of bombs.

COMMISSIONER EDWARD MULROONEY INSPECTING RECRUITS AT CAMP MULROONEY, PELHAM BAY PARK, SEPTEMBER 4, 1931. Commissioner Mulrooney is shown here on a two-hour inspection of this Bronx-based summer camp named in his honor. It was training 325 police rookies at the time. The police department established a foothold here from facilities that had been built by the Navy during World War I.

RECRUITS RECEIVING .32 CALIBER FIREARMS TRAINING AT CAMP MULROONEY, C. 1931. A Police Pistol Practice School was established shortly after the city's consolidation in 1898. In the 1930s, the department found City Island and Pelham Bay Park to be good locations for practice shooting due to their remote sites, which were both a safe distance away from residential neighborhoods. Just south of the park, the NYPD later established a large shooting range at Rodman's Neck in 1960.

RESCUING A HORSE, 1931. The Emergency Service Unit (ESU) was often called in on water rescues and not only for human beings. Here, ESU, with the help of a tow truck, rescues a horse that fell off a pier. To accomplish this rescue, ESU had to go into the water and slip the harness under the frightened animal.

EMERGENCY SERVICE UNIT AT PRACTICE, 1931. Even after making it through academy, continued on-the-job training was enormously important. This is the 19th Emergency Service Unit practicing medical treatment at their station in Bayside, Queens.

Spring 3100

January, 1935

POLICE

SERVICE PATIENCE and COURTESY

POLICE DEPARTMENT MAGAZINE *SPRING 3100*, 1935. Still published today, *Spring 3100* put out its first issue in 1930 at the directive of Commissioner Grover Whalen. Over the decades, it has been a vital resource to members of service in the department, to historians of police work, and to other New Yorkers. It took its name from the department's headquarters telephone number.

MAYOR FIORELLO LAGUARDIA AND COMMISSIONER LEWIS VALENTINE AT AWARDS CEREMONY, 1936. It was a partnership built on reform politics and a demand for excellence. Mayor Fiorello LaGuardia and his Police Commissioner Lewis Valentine had an extremely close working relationship throughout the mayor's long tenure. LaGuardia approved of Valentine's tough, no-nonsense measures, not only directed toward gangsters but also to those in the police department he felt were not doing their job. In his autobiography, Valentine estimated that in his first six years on the job he dismissed 300 officers and rebuked more than 4,000.

LEWIS VALENTINE, C. 1944. Valentine was the longest-serving commissioner of the NYPD in the 20th century. His mettle was tested, as the department was fighting a battle with organized crime and sorely undernourished resources during the Depression and World War II.

COMMISSIONER VALENTINE SPEAKING AT HOLY NAME COMMUNION BREAKFAST, ASTOR HOTEL, MARCH 22, 1942. Although the department took a tougher line toward discipline in the 1930s and 1940s, it also expanded its rewards for excellent service. Commissioner Valentine, shown speaking, awarded 23 medals for bravery at this meeting. The annual Holy Name Communion Breakfast was held at the Hotel Astor and attended by 3,000 people.

DISPOSING OF CRIMINAL WEAPONS AND SLOT MACHINES, C. 1935. The NYPD threw many captured weapons and other items used by criminals into the Atlantic Ocean and the Long Island Sound, not far from Mayor Fiorello LaGuardia's summer home at Eaton's Neck. This practice was ended in 1973 when the department began melting weapons down instead.

INSPECTING A RADIO MOTOR PATROL CAR, 1937. RMPs (Radio Motor Patrol cars) at first only received radio transmission from the department radio station, WPEG. Even in this limited capacity, the department quickly found the RMPs to be extraordinarily successful. In 1937, RMPs were also given the power to transmit as well as receive messages from the Communications Bureau. In this photograph, a group of men who were in New York attending a police convention is given a chance to inspect one of these vehicles up close. It was not until 1950 that the entire fleet of RMPs was equipped with two-way radios.

SPRING 3100 CARTOON, 1932. A cartoonist's interpretation of criminal reaction to the rise of RMPs is seen here. Between February 23 and August 8, 1932, a total of 377 arrests were attributed to the new communication system.

"We're finished"

OFFICERS IN AN EMERGENCY SERVICE TRUCK, 1938. Introduced in 1925, these dark blue emergency service trucks were capable of traveling more than 60 miles per hour and contained fire axes, acetylene torches, lifelines, stretchers, a rope cannon, and many other tools. The versatile vehicles were designed to respond to any kind of emergency, from riots to train wrecks.

CHILDREN AND POLICE OFFICER AT STREET CLOSURE, C. 1935. As traffic increased on city streets in the late 1920s, the police designated certain areas as "play streets," where motor vehicles were prohibited during daytime. The danger was real; 48 children under the age of 16 were killed by cars while roller-skating from 1929 through 1933. These days, crossing guards who are civilian employees of the department cover school crossings.

MOTORCYCLE SQUAD ESCORTING PRES. FRANKLIN DELANO ROOSEVELT, 1936. Motorcycle policemen have handled many historic escorts for presidents and other dignitaries visiting New York City over the decades. Roosevelt visited the city numerous times in 1936 for campaign appearances and the dedication of the Triborough Bridge. (Courtesy of Bronx Historical Society.)

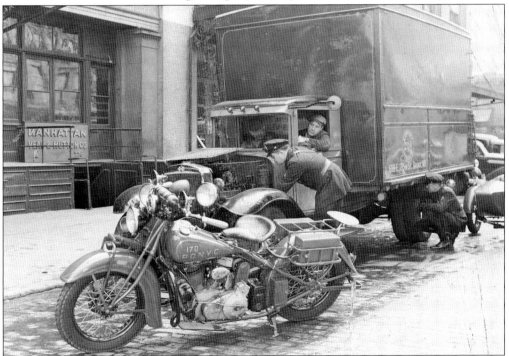

HIGHWAY SAFETY STOP, 1937. The Motorcycle Squad did more than provide escorts and catch speeders. They also responded to accident scenes to investigate and reconstruct the incident, especially if the accident was fatal, and they inspected trucks passing through the city, looking for equipment violations, such as defective brakes. Here, members of the Motorcycle Squad perform a safety check on a truck.

SCENES FROM THE 65TH PRECINCT, BROOKLYN, C. 1935. By the 1930s, many precinct station houses were in a state of aging disrepair. That decade and the one that followed were marked by the construction of many new police station houses with expanded, new facilities.

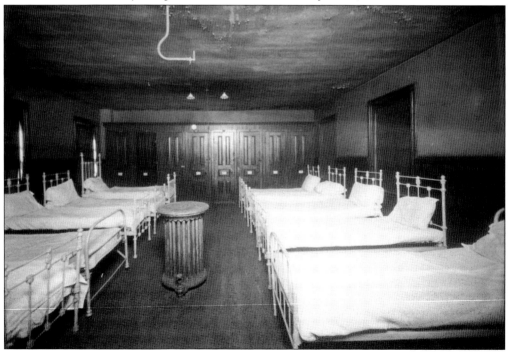

NEW STATION HOUSE OPENING, 110TH PRECINCT, FORTY-THIRD AVENUE, 1940. Located at 94-41 Forty-third Avenue in Elmhurst, Queens, this station house was opened in a ceremony by Mayor LaGuardia in January 1940. Constructed for $100,000, it replaced an older building located at Broadway and Justice Street.

PORTRAIT OF THE 23RD PRECINCT, 1936. Since the 1870s, a treasured memento found in every station house was the group portrait. It was ideally everyone assigned to the command, or squad, standing in front of the "house." One difficulty was getting everyone together to take the photograph. The photographer of this portrait overcame that obstacle by taking individual pictures of the officers and merging them together in one large montage.

Lt. John H.F. Cordes, 1939. The only officer to win the NYPD's Medal of Honor twice, John Cordes recorded 250 to 300 arrests per year in the 1920s. Unbelievably relentless, his first medal was awarded after he stopped a cigar store holdup and was shot five times. "I don't drink, I don't smoke, I don't play the races," he once said. "My only fun is putting these hoods in the box." In 1949, after 34 years on the job, he retired from the Detective Bureau as a lieutenant.

Police Officer Milton Wolf, c. 1936. Milton Wolf (1900–1999) was one of the first Jewish patrolmen to walk a beat in Sheepshead Bay. He was also an early participant in the Shomrim Society, a fraternal organization for Jewish police officers. The New York City Police Museum owns Wolf's unpublished autobiography, which provides a dramatic account of his experiences as a police officer in the Prohibition years and the difficulties of anti-Semitism.

Group of Drug Smugglers Arrested after Gun Battle with Police, 1939. Three men charged with smuggling $50,000 worth of opium answered questions proposed by the city's assistant district attorney, Paul Seiderman. One police officer was shot and wounded in the effort to capture the men.

Two-and-a-Half-Year-Old Allen Cohen Being Carried Out of the 181st Street Fort Washington Avenue Subway Station, 1940. Allen Cohen was the son and grandson of New York City police officers. In 1940, he wandered away from his mother and fell down escalator steps to the bottom of the subway station. Here, an unidentified officer is removing him from the station.

POLICEWOMEN AT THE NEW YORK WORLD'S FAIR, 1940. Police Academy graduation and swearing in ceremonies were often held at public venues. This helped to send a message to the community that the department was constantly expanding and becoming integrated into daily urban life. The 1940 class of policewomen were sworn in at the Government Zone area of the 1939–1940 New York World's Fair. This class included the first woman to become a chief, Gertrude Schimmel.

WOMEN SHARPSHOOTERS WITH COMMISSIONER VALENTINE, C. 1940. Police pistol tournaments were very popular in the 1930s and 1940s for both patrolmen and women. The NYPD sent both groups to the annual International Police Pistol Tournament, which was sponsored by New York newspapers. Eva Hanson, Adelaide Knowles, and Louise Wagner were frequent champions in the women's division. These women are posing with the *NY Mirror* trophy and Commissioner Valentine outside his office at headquarters on Centre Street.

PATROLMEN'S BENEVOLENT ASSOCIATION DELEGATES AT INDIAN HEAD HOTEL, PLATTE CLOVE, 1938. Built for $500,000 in 1926, the Indian Head Hotel became a well-appointed home away from home for officers and their families visiting the large Catskills recreation camp for the NYPD. The hotel replaced Indian Head Lodge in Platte Clove, Greene County, which had burned down in 1924. The entire property remained an important recreation center for decades. After the police left it, the hotel eventually became a religious residence owned by the Catskill Bruderhof.

BOMB SCENE AT THE NEW YORK WORLD'S FAIR, FLUSHING, 1940. Bomb Squad detectives Joseph Lynch and Ferdinand Socha died while attempting to defuse a bomb that had been placed inside the British Pavilion at the New York World's Fair. The city had responded to hundreds of bomb threats during the early years of war in Europe. The tragic loss of Detectives Lynch and Socha undoubtedly saved many other innocent lives and led to new methods in bomb disposal. (Courtesy of AP.)

LaGuardia-Pyke Bomb Truck, 1941. The New York World's Fair bombing inspired the design of this massive mobile bomb containment unit. Mayor Fiorello LaGuardia had the initial idea for a truck that could transport unexploded bombs to isolated spots for detonation. Lt. James Pyke perfected the design with the police department's technical laboratory, and it was successfully tested at Bergen Beach, Brooklyn.

Exploded LaGuardia-Pyke Bomb Truck, c. 1942. The trucks could withstand the explosive force of up to 24 sticks of dynamite and were designed to contain shrapnel but not gases. Resting upon the chassis of an eight-ton General Motors truck, the beehive-shaped carrier was woven together like a basket but with 5/8-inch-thick steel cables, which were also used as stringers for the Manhattan Bridge.

Five

THE MODERN NYPD EMERGES
1945–1980

In 1946, the mayor's office was occupied, for the first time, by a former police officer. William O'Dwyer had begun his career in public service across the East River from city hall, patrolling the Brooklyn waterfront precinct. Now, in his new position, he had his work cut out for him. The department desperately needed new officers and modernization. Fortunately, in the decades to come, advancements were made in the areas of personnel, training, and technological innovation.

Over time, the city increased the total number of police officers from 14,800 in 1946 to 23,590 by 1957 and, eventually, 30,000 in 1975. Meanwhile, policing New York City streets in the postwar years was supported by new tools and tactics. Radio Motor Patrol cars (RMPs) became increasingly important to postwar police work. Consequently, many officers were shifted away from traditional foot patrols. While there were downsides to this transition, RMPs dramatically extended the range of police officers. Other significant technological milestones in the first several decades after World War II included the introduction of handheld mobile two-way radio communication, the 911 call system, and computer-aided dispatch by 1969.

These advances demanded an increasingly well-trained individual. The department raised educational requirements in the 1950s and 1960s. Classes and physical training at the Police Academy became more rigorous, and in 1954, a police science program for prospective officers was introduced at the Baruch branch of City College. Reorganization extended well beyond training; squads for special homicide, robbery, and burglary were all created in the Detective Bureau. Meanwhile, department personnel grew increasingly more diverse, with a rising number of African Americans and women entering the uniform patrol by the early 1970s.

The city faced increasing tumult in the 1960s and the early 1970s, a time of great social and economic upheaval. The police department grappled with surging new threats and an increase in all violent crime. There were also riots and massive antiwar protests, growing tensions between minorities and police, and turbulence in every borough. Harlem exploded in a 1964 summer riot, but New York City was the only major American city to prevent further turmoil in the wake of Martin Luther King's assassination in 1968. An exploding drug trade posed huge tactical and ethical challenges. Eventually, allegations of systemic police corruption culminated in the Knapp Commission of 1973, which instituted important new reforms.

WILLIAM O'DWYER SPEAKING AT GROUND-BREAKING CEREMONY OF UNITED NATIONS, 1947. In 1946, William O'Dwyer became the first former police officer to be elected mayor of New York City. With $23.35 in his pocket, he had arrived in New York from County Mayo, Ireland, in 1910. The onetime candidate for the priesthood joined the department in 1917. While a patrolman, he graduated from Fordham Law School, which he attended at night. He left the department in 1923 to practice law, eventually becoming a judge.

PATROLMAN PHILIP FITZPATRICK, MOUNTED SQUAD NO. 1, c. 1945. One of the first officers to lay down their lives in the postwar years, Patrolman Philip Fitzpatrick once wrote an eerily prophetic poem, stating that when a policeman "kisses his wife and children goodbye, there's the chance he will see them no more." On May 20, 1947, Fitzpatrick and a fellow patrolman, both off-duty, disrupted a robbery on the Upper East Side. Fitzpatrick was shot while grappling with one of the thieves and later died.

JOHN CORCORAN AND MEMBERS OF HARBOR PATROL, c. 1948. John Corcoran (second from right) was a pilot for the Harbor Patrol from 1915 until 1954. In the early 1920s, he regulated boat traffic at Newtown Creek, a job so vital to the smooth operations of New York's waterways that the press dubbed him "Lord Admiral of Newton Creek." Corcoran was involved in many rescues over the years.

STUDENTS INSIDE POLICE ACADEMY CLASSROOM, C. 1955. As the size of the Police Academy classes grew after World War II, officials enhanced their training facilities and curriculum. The academy affiliated itself with the Baruch School of Public Administration at City College and formed associate- and master-level programs that were a forerunner to John Jay College of Criminal Justice.

THE HOURLY RING, c. 1950. In the days before two-way radios, a patrolman had to use the call box on his post to signal the station house. This call would inform the station of his well-being and of assignments designated for his post. Here, a lonely officer makes his "ring" on a quiet stretch of Broadway at Ninety-eighth Street during a snowstorm in the 1950s.

EMERGENCY SERVICE UNIT HELPING IN BODY RECOVERY, c. 1950. When victims of fatal accidents or crimes are found in inaccessible locations, ESU is often called upon to assist. This photograph shows ESU helping police from the 25th Precinct recover a body.

RESCUE OF CHILD, C. 1955. ESU personnel was handling 30,000 emergency calls a year by the late 1950s. A variety of emergencies—from dramatic rescues like this to securing life belts for people attempting to commit suicide—required an enormous tool kit. ESU patrol vehicles were stocked with nearly 75 different tools, ranging from hydraulic jacks to oxygen resuscitators.

POLICE CAR AT TRAFFIC STOP, 1955. Despite progress in controlling traffic in previous decades, by the early 1950s, New York City still had the highest death rate per registered vehicle among major American cities. The city brought renewed effort to reducing traffic violations, monitoring speeders with radar equipment, and setting up more traffic checkpoints than ever before.

POLICE HELICOPTER, C. 1950. In the late 1940s, the police department began transitioning from fixed-wing aircrafts to helicopters, which gave them more versatility and the ability to monitor traffic, beaches, and ground-level emergencies at lower altitudes. By the late 1950s, the department was using Bell 47-J helicopters, which traveled at speeds up to 100 miles per hour.

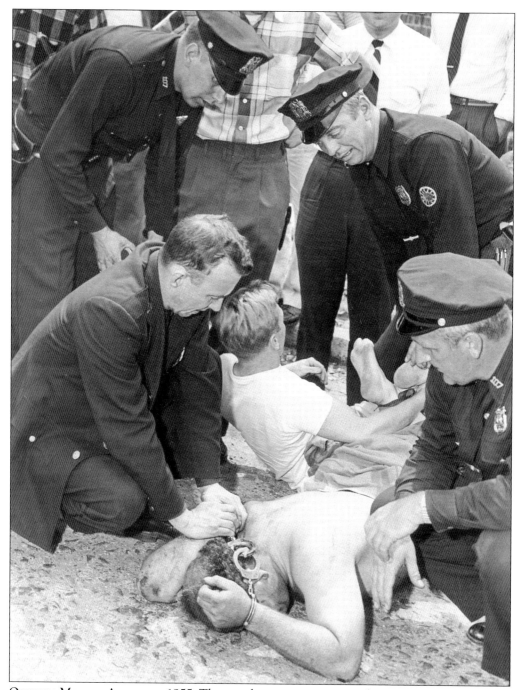

Officers Making Arrest, c. 1955. The way that crime was reported in New York City changed in 1950 when the responsibility for record keeping was moved from the precincts to headquarters. As a result, crime statistics were recorded more consistently, one of the reasons behind a precipitous rise in postwar crime numbers.

WILLIE SUTTON'S MUG SHOT, 1952. A master of disguise and an escape artist, William "Willie" Sutton made off with an estimated $2 million during his career. Once asked why he robbed banks, he allegedly responded, "Because that's where the money is." Sutton's career ended with his arrest in New York City in 1952.

GEORGE METESKY, "THE MAD BOMBER," 1957. From 1940 to 1956, George Metesky planted 33 bombs in public places across the city in an effort to exact revenge on his former employer, Con Edison. Fifteen people were wounded, and New Yorkers were terrorized. When detectives determined there was a Con Ed connection, they reviewed thousands of personnel files before finally finding a connection to Metesky, who was arrested in 1957.

NYPD Officer in Bomb Suit Body Armor, c. 1955. The NYPD developed one of its first bomb suits in the 1950s. It was distributed amongst the borough detective commands, Emergency Service Unit, and the Bomb Squad. The armor was made of heat-treated metal plates wrapped in nylon cloth.

TWO OFFICERS LISTENING TO CITIZEN, C. 1960. In 1960, more than 75 percent of the members of the police department were patrolmen. They performed eight-hour tours in three five-day cycles. After working five late tours—12:00 a.m. to 8:00 a.m.—they were given 56 hours off and then began late afternoon to evening shifts and finally day tours.

OFFICER TAKING NOTES FOR INVESTIGATION, C. 1960. Technology effected gradual, subtle shifts in the police officer's job in the years after World War II. As officers responded more to dispatchers rather than directly to citizens, strategies became more reactive. However, on-the-street interviews, like the one pictured here, were still vital to policing.

POLICEMAN AT CALL BOX, C. 1960. Rapid mobilization plans were developed in the late 1950s to deal with large-scale disorder. Part of the plan was to recall off-duty police officers. Cops responded to different locations, depending on where they were at the time of the deployment. For example, officers living on Long Island but assigned to a precinct in Manhattan may have been directed to report to a Queens precinct. Here, an off-duty officer, with police armband, is teamed with a uniformed officer. They are calling into the station house for instructions.

PROTESTERS OF KHRUSHCHEV AND CASTRO, 1960. In late September 1960, the NYPD faced the enormous challenge of protecting Soviet premier Nikita Khrushchev and Cuban prime minister Fidel Castro during their visit to the United Nations. While the State Department limited the leaders' travel to Manhattan, the department ramped up an unprecedented level of protection. Thousands of officers from the other boroughs were brought in.

KHRUSHCHEV AND CASTRO VISIT UNITED NATIONS, 1960. While the tensions ran high with enormous numbers of protesters, pickets were generally peaceful. Groups who opposed the visit (and the visit of other controversial leaders, like the dictatorial president of Yugoslavia, Marshal Tito) were diverse and included everyone from Cuban expatriates to members of the International Longshoreman's Association.

ST. PATRICK'S DAY PARADE, 1961.
A favorite of New Yorkers since 1762, the St. Patrick's Day Parade was also popular with members of the police department, since a majority of the force was Irish American during much of the department's history. The Emerald Society, the nation's first for a police department, was formed in 1953. Here, members of the society prepare to march up Fifth Avenue on March 17, 1961.

EMERALD SOCIETY MEMBER AT PULASKI PARADE, 1963. When the department's band was dismantled in 1953, the Emerald Society Pipe and Drum Band became the de facto official band of the department. Here, a member of the band prepares to march in the 1963 Pulaski Parade.

SHOMRIM SOCIETY NEWSLETTER, 1963.
One of the oldest religious groups in the NYPD, the Shomrim Society was founded in 1924 for Jewish police officers. Its original purpose was to combat the anti-Semitism that Jewish officers experienced and to raise the numbers of Jewish policemen, who constituted less than one percent of the force at the time. Some 70 years later, the fruits of the society's work was borne out when Howard Safir became the NYPD's first Jewish police commissioner.

CHARITY • FRIENDSHIP • PROTECTION

SHOMRIM NEWS

Founded
October 16, 1924

Incorporated
February 28, 1925

The SHOMRIM SOCIETY, Inc.
POLICE DEPARTMENT of the CITY OF NEW YORK

Affiliated with Council of Jewish Organizations in Civil Service and National Conference of Shomrim Societies

VOL. 39   NOVEMBER, 1963   No. 18

FROM RIGHT TO LEFT: PRESIDENT LOUIS A. FRANK, RABBI JACOB M. SABLE, CHAPLAIN ISIDORE FRANK, CHIEF INSPECTOR MICHAEL LEDDEN, POLICE COMMISSIONER MICHAEL J. MURPHY.

WIN A FREE WEEK-END AT THE CONCORD

Monday, Nov. 18, 1963, 8 p. m.
HOTEL RIVERSIDE
73rd STREET — WEST OF BROADWAY

344

COMMANDER SEALY OUTSIDE THE 28TH PRECINCT, C. 1964.
No police officer did more to quell racial violence in New York City neighborhoods in the 1960s than Lloyd George Sealy. The son of Barbadian immigrants, Sealy became a lieutenant in 1959. After receiving acclaim as a peacemaker during the Harlem riot of 1964, Sealy was chosen to command the 28th Precinct. After completing his policing career, Sealy joined the faculty at John Jay College. The school library now bears his name.

AERIAL VIEW OF RODMAN'S NECK OUTDOOR FIRING RANGE, C. 1965. Rodman's Neck opened in June 1960 as a firing range that provided basic instruction to new recruits and additional training to NYPD veterans. The sounds of gunfire and explosions were not new sounds to this small neck that juts into Eastchester Bay. It was previously home to Revolutionary War skirmishes, a Navy training center, and an Army rocket base.

MANHATTAN COMMAND AND CONTROL CENTER, 1968. This was the command and control center for all boroughs, located in the old gym at 240 Centre Street. Community crime reporting and instantaneous communication with police dispatchers was a new development for the NYPD in the 1960s. In 1964, residents were given the first citywide emergency phone number, 440-1234. In 1968, the 911 call system was introduced nationwide, and New York City became the first major American city to adopt it.

**POLICEWOMAN AT CALL BOX,
c. 1968.** Starting in the 1920s,
select civilians were issued call
box keys. The locked call box
could only be accessed by these
citizens, whose names and address
were published and well known
within the neighborhood. By the
time this photograph was taken,
all call boxes were unlocked and
equipped with signs instructing
the public in their use.

**FRANK SERPICO TESTIFYING
BEFORE KNAPP COMMISSION,
1970.** Frank Serpico was the
plainclothes detective who
became a central figure during the
Knapp Commission's investigation
in 1970. Along with several other
policemen, he provided evidence
of corruption that shocked the
city and led to a department-
wide reorganization. His story
was later recounted in a book
and a movie starring Al Pacino.
(Courtesy of *New York Times*;
photograph by Librado Romero.)

LINE-OF-DUTY FUNERAL, 1971. In this photograph, officers of the Ceremonial Unit, wearing the old-style winter blouse commonly referred to as the "choker," act as pallbearers for a line-of-duty funeral. Officers killed in the line of duty are honored by the NYPD with a full inspector's funeral. Coordinated by the department's Ceremonial Unit, the funeral includes a processional, motorcycle escort, color guard, and a tribute by the NYPD Emerald Society Pipe and Drum Band. Fellow officers attending funerals wear full dress uniforms.

HEADQUARTERS AT POLICE PLAZA, C. 1975. Critics of the Police Headquarters at 240 Centre Street stated that it was outdated before it was finished. Plans for a new building were drafted in 1928, but it was not until 1973 that a new headquarters was opened. Built at a cost of $58 million, the building's plans boasted amenities like air-conditioning, a helipad, underground parking, and a second-floor cafeteria. (Courtesy of *Spring 3100*.)

Gertrude D.T. Schimmel's Promotion to Deputy Chief, 1978. Many women paved the way for future generations of female police officers. Gertrude Schimmel was perhaps the most significant of these path breakers. She started her career as a policewoman on June 5, 1940, and worked her way up to be promoted to sergeant in 1965 and captain in 1971. With future Police Commissioner Benjamin Ward, she helped organize the experimental use of women in uniformed patrol in 1972, before being promoted to deputy chief six years later.

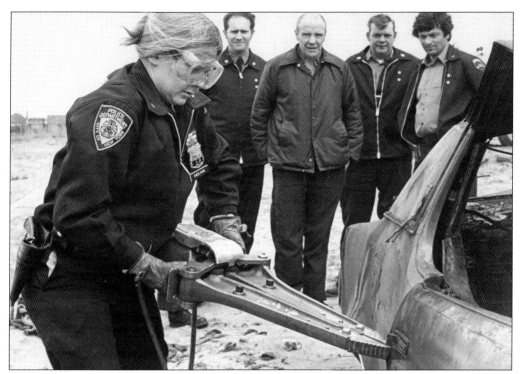

PHOTOGRAPHS OF HELEN KNEDLEHANS, EMERGENCY SERVICE OFFICER AND INSTRUCTOR, AND PEGGY O'SHAUGHNESSY, 40TH PRECINCT, C. 1977. For generations, women had held limited jobs within the NYPD. But the 1970s saw the beginning of a breakthrough in their full-fledged involvement in all services and areas of duty in the department. The transition was not smooth, nor was it fast. But it held promise for their rapid advancement in decades to come. "All of the women, I'm sure, felt that they were constantly being watched and challenged," Helen Knedlehans, shown above, told photographer Jane Hoffer, who documented women's rise in the department. She went on to say, "Every woman out on the street has to prove she can do the job." Peggy O'Shaughnessy is pictured below. (Both, photograph by Jane Hoffer.)

COURTROOM PAINTING BY AGGIE KENNY OF COMPETENCY HEARING FOR DAVID BERKOWITZ, 1977. After killing six people and wounding seven others, David Berkowitz was captured on August 10, 1977. Berkowitz had called himself the "Son of Sam" in his public letters and had targeted young couples and women in early morning hours with a .44-caliber gun, which the NYPD was able to forensically match to bullets. Officers unraveled the killer's identity by tracing Berkowitz to the last crime scene in Brooklyn through a parking ticket.

.44 CALIBER KILLER CAPTURED

ommissioner Michael J. Codd congratu-
tes newly promoted Deputy Inspector
seph Borrelli, left, and Deputy Chief
mothy J. Dowd. The officers received
attlefield promotions" for directing the
on of Sam investigation.

TWENTY-FIVE PROMOTED FOR SON OF SAM ARREST

COMMISSIONER MICHAEL CODD WITH TWO OFFICERS WHO RECEIVED PROMOTIONS FOR ROLE IN "SON OF SAM" INVESTIGATION, 1977. The Homicide Task Force carried out an exhaustive effort to uncover the murderer, reviewing thousands of public tips and conducting special patrols and stakeouts. Ultimately, 25 police officers were promoted for their relentless and successful dedication to stopping the ".44-Caliber Killer." (Courtesy of *Spring 3100*.)

POLICE UNIFORM, C. 1975. The 1970s NYPD uniform consisted of two innovations: a light-blue shirt and an arm patch. In 1969, it was announced that police officers would trade their traditional dark-blue worsted shirts for a wash-and-wear light-blue model. In 1970, the department created an arm patch to be worn on the right shoulder to further distinguish NYPD officers from those of other agencies.

DRIVING OVER THE TRIBOROUGH BRIDGE, 1978. The new police cars introduced in 1973 had a variety of new features that went beyond color schemes. They were equipped with custom-made reflective license plates, an electronic siren, and a public address system.

Six

THE NYPD TODAY
1980–2011

Despite it all—new threats, tough economies, and towering responsibilities—the New York City Police Department evolved to meet the challenges of today. The department has become an international model for other law enforcement agencies, developing cutting-edge crime-reduction tactics and facing the global challenge of terrorism with effective new strategies.

The early 1970s were a difficult time for the NYPD and the entire city. A fiscal crisis led to thousands of police officers being laid off in the mid-1970s, many of whom were eventually hired back. However, as department resources remained static, crime rose steadily in the 1980s, especially during the crack cocaine epidemic. By 1990, homicides reached an all-time annual high of 2,245. In response, New York instituted the "Safe City, Safe Streets" program in 1991. It eventually raised the size of the NYPD to 38,310 officers. The infusion of personnel coincided with the beginning of a historic fall in crime that continues through today. Since 1990, the seven major index crimes have been driven down by more than 80 percent overall. In 1994, the Compstat system was created. It utilized electronic mapping and weekly meetings with precinct commanders to analyze crime trends and ensure an effective response. The department subsequently rode an enormous wave of success, as crime fell by 40 percent from 1993 to 1997 alone.

With the attacks of September 11, the mission of the NYPD changed forever. Now, in addition to fighting crime, the department was charged with protecting New York from another terrorist attack. The NYPD created a new Counterterrorism Bureau, the first of its kind in the nation, and dedicated 1,000 police officers to this function. In addition, the Intelligence Division was restructured to gather and analyze information globally about terrorism and crime.

Despite devoting substantial resources to counterterrorism, the NYPD has continued to drive crime down by 34 percent in the 10 years since 2001. That includes the lowest number of homicides recorded in a single year (471 in 2009) since 1963. Meanwhile, in cooperation with its federal partners, the NYPD has deterred 14 terrorist plots against New York since September 11.

Another factor that has helped the NYPD meet the demands of its new mission is its unprecedented diversity. In 2006, for the first time, the rank of police officer became majority-minority. Since that time, the department has hired officers born in 88 different countries representing dozens of ethnicities, nationalities, and faiths. In addition to helping the NYPD work well with the communities it serves, this increasing diversity has allowed it to build a foreign linguist program with more than 800 registered speakers of 60 different languages and a cyber unit to monitor potential threats on the Internet.

POLICE COMMISSIONER BENJAMIN WARD, 1984. The first African American police commissioner in New York City history, Commissioner Benjamin Ward was appointed by Mayor Edward Koch after more than 30 years in law enforcement. A native of Brooklyn, he took on a series of leadership roles in the NYPD and New York City Corrections in the 1970s and 1980s. Ward's tenure (1984–1989) came during a difficult era of rising crime, a crack epidemic, and racial tensions. Through it all, he maintained a calm command and increased the hiring of black police officers by 17 percent, Hispanics by 60 percent, and women by 85 percent.

HELICOPTER HIGH OVER NEW YORK, C. 1985. As technology and capabilities have advanced, so have the responsibilities of the Aviation Unit. Today's helicopters carry infrared sensors and surveillance equipment, which support the efforts of antiterrorism, the tracking of criminals, and search and rescue.

PHYSICAL TRAINING, 1985. After Ward's appointment as commissioner in 1984, the department undertook several new training initiatives. Beyond a new emphasis on community-oriented policing, the physical fitness requirements were updated. The new fitness model measured body fat, flexibility, and strength, mandating benchmarks prior to patrol assignments.

COMMISSIONER LEE BROWN VISITS MEMBERS OF 70TH PRECINCT, 1989. Lee Brown was police commissioner from 1990 to 1992. During that time, he instituted a series of reforms under the rubric of "community policing." Brown spoke frequently of having his police officers be "part of, and not apart from, the community." After leaving the NYPD, Brown went on to become the first African American mayor of Houston. (Courtesy of *Spring 3100*.)

OFFICER FROM 40TH PRECINCT INVOLVED WITH OPERATION SAFE CORRIDOR, 1990. More uniformed officers were placed on foot patrols, and the Community Patrol Officer Program (CPOP, initiated in 1984) was enlarged and granted more resources. (Courtesy of *Spring 3100*.)

BOY RESCUED FROM NEAR TOP OF MIDTOWN MANHATTAN PARKING GARAGE, 1991. Captured in this photograph taken by a passerby near the Port Authority Terminal are Emergency Service personnel saving a child who had threatened to jump. (Both, courtesy of Lee Herterich.)

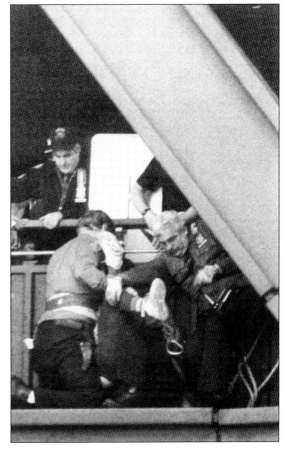

POLICE COMMISSIONER WILLIAM BRATTON AND MAYOR RUDY GIULIANI WITH DEPARTMENT PERSONNEL, 1993. The principal leaders of the NYPD's reformed approach in the mid-1990s were Police Commissioner William Bratton (third from left) and Mayor Rudy Giuliani (sixth from left). Already declining when former federal district attorney Giuliani became mayor in 1993, crime continued to go down precipitously during his years in office. Bratton came to New York after serving as superintendent for the Boston Police Department. He brought a business management style to his office. Resigning in 1996, Bratton later became chief for the Los Angeles Police Department. (Courtesy of *Spring 3100*.)

POLICE COMMISSIONER HOWARD SAFIR (CENTER) AT A PARADE ON BROADWAY AFTER THE NEW YORK YANKEES WORLD SERIES VICTORY, c. 1999. Commissioner Howard Safir was the first person in history to serve as both fire commissioner and police commissioner of New York City. During Safir's tenure, 1996–2000, crime in New York continued to decline due to the deployment of successful crime-reduction strategies and the increased use of new technologies, such as DNA testing.

BOMB SQUAD OFFICERS REVIEWING WORLD TRADE CENTER BOMBING BLAST SCENE, 1993. On February 26, 1993, a 1,336-pound truck bomb exploded below the North Tower of the World Trade Center. Six people were killed and more than 1,000 were injured in the attack, which gave the NYPD an increased awareness of the vulnerability of the city to terrorist attacks. (Courtesy of *Spring 3100*.)

View of World Trade Center Attack from under Brooklyn Bridge, September 11, 2001. The terrorist attack on New York City claimed the lives of 23 New York City police officers and 37 Port Authority Police Department officers and commanders. Despite the tragic loss, the day is also documented with many incidents of heroism as the police department responded to a rapidly changing picture on the ground. In the aftermath of September 11, the department would change its operations enormously. Sadly, the ultimate sacrifices of that day continue: as of the publishing of this book, nearly 50 NYPD officers have died due to long-term health consequences from their work in the recovery and cleanup effort.

VIEW OF BROOKLYN BRIDGE, 2005. One of the immediate concerns of New Yorkers and the NYPD in the days and months after September 11 was protecting the city from further attack. With its many iconic landmarks and high-profile symbols of the nation's financial and political system, the city remained a target. In 2003, Iyman Faris was arrested after plotting to destroy the Brooklyn Bridge. In the years since September 11, the NYPD has prevented 14 other terrorist plots. (Courtesy of *Spring 3100*.)

MARKER FOR JET FUEL PIPELINE SUPPLYING JFK AIRPORT, 2007. In 2007, four men affiliated with a radical Islamic group were arrested in New York and Trinidad, charged with attempting to bomb John F. Kennedy Airport's pipeline and fuel tanks. The NYPD and the FBI worked together to bring the suspects, who were under surveillance for a year, to justice. (AP Photo/Rick Maiman.)

MEMBERS OF THE NYPD EMERGENCY SERVICE UNIT AT A CHECKPOINT, 2007. The ESU member in this photograph is using a radiation detection device to check a truck at a security checkpoint on Broadway and Canal Street. (AP Photo/Mary Altaffer.)

Najibullah Zazi Being Escorted off an NYPD Helicopter, 2009. This photograph shows Zazi after extradition from Denver, Colorado. In early 2010, Zazi admitted to a plot to bomb New York City subways. He was convicted and sentenced to prison. (AP Photo/NYPD.)

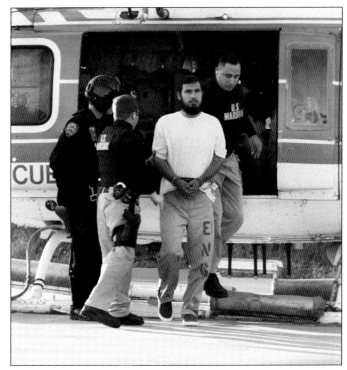

Preventing the Bronx Synagogue Bombings, 2009. Four men were arrested in 2009 for attempting to bomb two Riverdale synagogues. The men had further plotted to shoot down a military aircraft at an upstate New York Air National Guard Base. All were convicted and sentenced to jail. (Courtesy of *Spring 3100*.)

POLICE COMMISSIONER RAYMOND W. KELLY BRIEFING NYPD OFFICIALS AND JOHN O. BRENNAN, ASSISTANT TO THE PRESIDENT FOR HOMELAND SECURITY AND COUNTERTERRORISM (CENTER RIGHT), 2009. This photograph illustrates the high level of cooperation between the NYPD and the federal government in the counterterrorist effort. At Police Headquarters, Commissioner Kelly is briefing officials about events surrounding the plot to bomb New York City commuter trains on September 11, 2009. (AP Photo/NYPD.)

BOMB SQUAD OFFICER WORKING ON SUV AT TIMES SQUARE, 2010. The NYPD prevented another serious attack when a potentially powerful bomb was placed in the SUV with its door open, seen at the right of this photograph, at Times Square on May 2, 2010. Officers recovered cans of gasoline, tanks of propane, fireworks, and electrical equipment to defuse the bomb. A 30-year-old man, Faisal Shahzad, was later arrested for the bombing attempt and is now in prison. (AP Photo/*Spring 3100.*)

POLICE COMMISSIONER RAYMOND W. KELLY WITH NYPD SEPTEMBER 11 FIRST RESPONDERS AND PRES. BARACK OBAMA, 2011. Commissioner Kelly has succeeded in driving crime in New York City to historic lows and also developed the NYPD's first-in-the-nation municipal Counterterrorism Bureau. Kelly has served twice as police commissioner, first from 1992 to 1994 and currently since 2002. Kelly has spent 43 years in the NYPD and served in several federal posts as well. He earned two law degrees and a master's in public administration from Harvard's Kennedy School. These photographs were taken during President Obama's historic visit to Police Headquarters in May 2011, which was when he thanked the NYPD officers who responded to the failed attempt to target Times Square with a car bomb earlier that month. (Above, courtesy AP; below, courtesy *Spring 3100*.)

HERCULES TEAM MEMBER NEAR TIMES SQUARE, 2004. Hercules Teams are made up of members of the Emergency Service Unit who have received highly specialized training. They pay unannounced visits to sensitive locations based on intelligence.

HERCULES TEAM MEMBERS, C. 2006. The visible presence of Hercules Teams works to dissuade terrorist surveillance. (Courtesy of *Spring 3100*.)

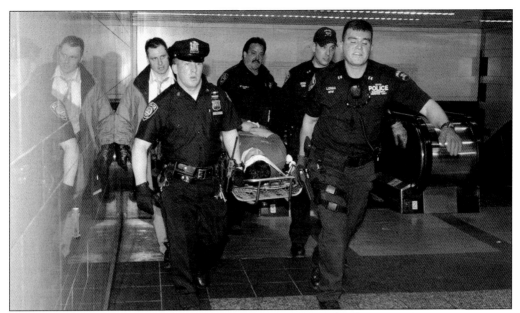

OFFICERS RESPOND TO A CRASH AT PENN STATION, 2004. The department's counterterrorism training has also given officers tools to respond to other, non-terror-related emergencies. In April 2004, an Amtrak train collided with the back of a Long Island Railroad train at Penn Station, causing hundreds of injuries.

NYPD'S INITIATION OF BAG CHECKS, 2005. The police department began a program to check bags and backpacks of subway riders after the London subway attacks in July 2005. The public is notified of the program ahead of time, and individuals are free to leave the subway station rather than submit to the search. Bags and packages are screened visually and with handheld detection equipment. (Courtesy of *Spring 3100.*)

NYPD SECURITY CHECKPOINT, 2005. Checkpoints are an essential counterterrorism tool. The searches are established for specific events, according to certain threat information, or around sensitive locations. They are also utilized at entry points into the city to ensure large commercial vehicles are not carrying unauthorized explosives or other hazardous materials.

INSIDE REAL TIME CRIME CENTER (RTCC), c. 2006. Opened in 2005, the Real Time Crime Center is staffed 24 hours a day by detectives who utilize sophisticated and comprehensive technology that supports the efforts of officers working in the field. Detectives at RTCC access the center's data warehouse, which contains billions of public and classified records. This information is then shared with detectives working in the field.

NYPD Intelligence Division at Work, 2005. The Intelligence Division analyzes threat information from around the world and applies it to the protection of New York City. The division utilizes the skills of civilian analysts, cyber detectives, and senior officers who are stationed overseas.

NYPD Shield Briefing, 2006. The Counterterrorism Bureau launched NYPD Shield in July 2005 to engage private security professionals in the work of counterterrorism. The program keeps its membership of 10,000 informed of possible terrorist threats.

MEMBERS OF OPERATION **TORCH,** GRAND CENTRAL STATION, 2010. TORCH, or Transit Operational Response with Canine and Heavy Weapons, supports efforts of the NYPD's Transit Bureau. This photograph was taken when security was increased as a precaution after a suicide bombing in Moscow's subway system in March 2010. (AP Photo/Kathy Willens.)

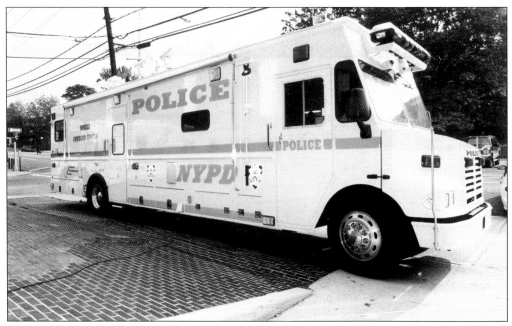

MOBILE COMMAND CENTER, 2006. These high-tech moving units are fully equipped with state-of-the-art audio and visual technology for the communications personnel and tactical officers inside.

MOBILE INTERDICTION OF RADIATION EMITTING MATERIAL (IREM) SYSTEM, 2007. The IREMs mounted to these trucks give readings on radioactive sources, and surveillance cameras document each vehicle, which get scanned. (Courtesy of *Spring 3100*.)

NYPD BOAT PATROLLING NEW YORK'S WATERS, 2006. Harbor Patrol has come a great distance from the rowboats and steam patrol of the late 19th century. The NYPD has many tools at its disposal to patrol the city's 578 miles of coastline, including several boats with Tactical Radiation Acquisition and Characterization Systems (TRACS), shown in the photograph above, that can reach speeds greater than 50 knots. (Courtesy of *Spring 3100*.)

USE OF HANDHELD DEVICES, 2006.
The NYPD has increasingly turned
toward handheld devices, which give
them enormous amounts of critical
data from the precincts, the Real Time
Crime Center, and Police Headquarters
as they needed it. Working in the field,
officers have at their fingertips such
usable information as criminal records,
gun permits, and other information.

**PUBLIC SAFETY
ANSWERING CENTER,
2006.** New York
City began its 911
call system dispatch
program in the
late 1960s, and it
has become the
public's most vital
lifeline through the
age of cell phone
technology. In 2006,
over 11 million calls
were answered at the
center, and operators
dispatched more
than 4.6 million
NYPD radio runs.

POLICE ACADEMY GRADUATION, 2008. The NYPD has ever increasingly come to reflect the demographics of the city it serves. In 2006, for the first time in its history, the department's police officer rank became majority-minority, with more African American, Latino, and Asian American officers than white. Today's graduates are tomorrow's leaders who will continue to write new chapters of New York's policing history.

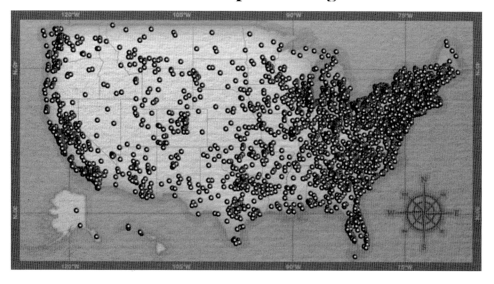